"With admirable courage to address d
ence routinely but rarely talk about, D
great gift to the mental health prof(
thought-provoking, and consistently cle ___ can elevate
treatment to higher levels of effectiveness. ..er language is careful and
even poetic at times making her clinical insights and case examples
especially powerful. Take the time to read this important book!"

Michael D. Yapko, PhD, *clinical psychologist and author of*
Depression is Contagious *and* The Discriminating Therapist

"Peebles has thrown a lifeline to all of us in the swamps of clinical
impasse. Radically integrative, *When Psychotherapy Feels Stuck*
embodies the author's respect for different theoretical orientations,
appreciation of neuroscientific discoveries, mastery of psychological
assessment, and extensive knowledge of both clinical and research
literatures. Her fluid, accessible writing is rich with clinical anec-
dotes, arresting metaphors, and the practical advice that comes only
from decades of experience. I learned a lot and recommend this book
to therapists of all backgrounds, levels of experience, clinical
settings, and theoretical orientations."

Nancy McWilliams, PhD, ABPP; *Rutgers Graduate School of*
Applied and Professional Psychology

"In this engaging new book, Mary Jo Peebles takes the reader on a
journey to the heart of stuckness. She uses neuroscientific findings,
psychoanalytic insight, and her own subjective experience to illuminate
how we all get stuck and how we might find a way out. Her prose is
poetic and jargon free, and the result is a deeply moving and
intellectually creative overview of what psychotherapy is all about. I
found her insights extremely useful in my work and you will too. I
highly recommend it to both therapists and potential patients."

Glen O. Gabbard, MD, *author of* Love and Hate
in the Analytic Setting

"A wealth of wisdom! Dr. Peebles has given us a gift that draws from
years of experience and a reading of diverse literatures. Her book is
paved with clinical insights and illustrations as she embraces and feels
into the experience of stuckness along dimensions of communication
and relationship, awareness and emotion, uncertainty and vulnerability, and ultimately meaning-making. Professionals of any experience level, from any theoretical orientation, and in any practice
modality will appreciate what she has written."

J. Christopher Muran, PhD, *Gordon F. Derner School of Psychology,*
Adelphi University; Icahn School of Medicine at Mount Sinai

When Psychotherapy Feels Stuck

Every therapist feels stuck at some point. Dr. Peebles offers ways of working with patients that clear openings for growth inside those stuck-places.

When Psychotherapy Feels Stuck integrates wisdom from multiple theoretical schools. It balances explicit, systematized frameworks for thinking with sensory-based metaphors. Chapters interweave empirical research with clinical vignettes to describe the power of language choices, tolerating not-knowing, risking relationship, and creating meaning.

Therapists from all theoretical backgrounds and experience levels will find something unexpected here that sparks hope and a fresh take when feeling stuck.

Mary Jo Peebles, PhD, ABPP, ABPH, is a psychoanalyst, therapist, writer, and teacher currently in private practice in Bethesda, Maryland.

When Psychotherapy
Feels Stuck

Mary Jo Peebles

Routledge
Taylor & Francis Group

NEW YORK AND LONDON

First published 2022
by Routledge
605 Third Avenue, New York, NY 10158

and by Routledge
2 Park Square, Milton Park, Abingdon, Oxon, OX14 4RN

Routledge is an imprint of the Taylor & Francis Group, an informa business

Library of Congress Cataloging-in-Publication Data
Names: Peebles, Mary Jo, author.
Title: When psychotherapy feels stuck / Mary Jo Peebles.
Description: New York : Routledge, 2021. | Includes bibliographical references and index. |
Identifiers: LCCN 2021012604 (print) | LCCN 2021012605 (ebook) | ISBN 9781138204287 (hardback) | ISBN 9781138204300 (paperback) | ISBN 9781315449043 (ebook)
Subjects: LCSH: Psychotherapy--Vocational guidance. | Psychotherapy--Practice.
Classification: LCC RC440.8 .P44 2021 (print) | LCC RC440.8 (ebook) | DDC 616.89/14023--dc23
LC record available at https://lccn.loc.gov/2021012604
LC ebook record available at https://lccn.loc.gov/2021012605

ISBN: 978-1-138-20428-7 (hbk)
ISBN: 978-1-138-20430-0 (pbk)
ISBN: 978-1-315-44904-3 (ebk)

DOI: 10.4324/9781315449043

Typeset in Sabon
by MPS Limited, Dehradun

...to my children

Contents

Author Biography

Mary Jo Peebles, PhD, ABPP, ABPH, is a graduate of Wellesley College and Case Western Reserve University. She completed a postdoctoral fellowship in systems approaches to child and family therapy at University of Texas Medical Branch Galveston and a postdoctoral fellowship in psychodynamic adult psychotherapy and diagnosis at Menninger in Topeka, Kansas. Peebles is a psychoanalyst, board certified in clinical psychology and psychological hypnosis, and has written and taught nationally and internationally in the areas of psychotherapy, trauma, and psychological testing. She is currently in private practice in Bethesda, Maryland.

Acknowledgments

Grateful acknowledgment is made for permission to reprint the following works:

Text excerpt from *Selections From the Living Series* [sculpture] by Jenny Holzer; 1989; Installed Minneapolis Sculpture Garden; Walker Art Center; Minneapolis, MN. © 2021 Jenny Holzer, member Artists Rights Society (ARS), New York. Reprinted by permission of ARSNY.

Excerpt from THE ONCE AND FUTURE KING by T.H. White, copyright © 1938, 1939, 1940, 1958 by T.H. White. Used by permission of G.P. Putnam's Sons, an imprint of Penguin Publishing Group, a division of Penguin Random House LLC. All rights reserved.

Excerpt from *101 Things I Wish I'd Known When I Started Using Hypnosis* by D. Ewin, Copyright © 2009. Reproduced by permission of Crown House Publishing Limited, Camarthen, Wales, UK.

Excerpt from PEACE IS EVERY STEP: THE PATH OF MINDFULNESS IN EVERYDAY LIFE by Thich Nhat Hanh, Copyright (c)1991 by Thich Nhat Hanh. Used by permission of Bantam Books, an imprint of Random House, a division of Penguin Random House LLC. All rights reserved.

Excerpt from *Notes On Memory and Desire* by W. Bion, Copyright © 2013. From Wilfred Bion: Los Angeles seminars and supervision by J. Aguayo and B. Malin (Eds.). Reproduced by permission of Taylor and Francis Group, LLC, a division of Informa plc.

Excerpt from A WAY OF BEING by Carl Rogers. Copyright © 1980 by Houghton Mifflin Harcourt Publishing Company, renewed 2008 by David E. Rogers and Natalie Rogers. Reprinted by permission of Houghton Mifflin Harcourt Publishing Company. All rights reserved.

Excerpt from "Negative process": A recurrently discovered and underestimated facet of therapeutic process and outcome in the individual psychotherapy of adults, Copyright © 1997. From *Clinical Psychology: Science and Practice*, volume 4, pp. 121–139, by J.L. Binder and H.H. Strupp. Rights held by the author. Reproduced by permission of author, J.L. Binder PhD.

Excerpts from *The Art of Racing in the Rain* by Garth Stein. Copyright © 2008 by Bright White Light, LLC. Used by permission of HarperCollins Publishers.

Grateful acknowledgment is made also to Routledge, an imprint of Taylor & Francis Group, its production staff, and to Anna Moore, Publisher, for shepherding this book from idea-conception to completion.

Several colleagues provided feedback on manuscript chapters. They were generous with their time, astute and sharp, and graced me with frankness and warmth: Sophia Coudenhove-Kalergi, LCSW; Jennifer Kennedy, MD; Colleen Kleiger, LCSW; Kathleen C. Kleiger, BFA; Tracy B. McGillivary, JD, LLM; and Rhonda Reinholtz, PhD.

A special thanks to Catherine Yochum, graphic designer, who used her gifts of empathy and synesthesia to create ingenious cover options.

Finally, I am indebted to Sydny Miner, whose editorial mind swiftly grasped and adroitly pared my message so it showed itself clearly. She was respectful and decisive. I consider her a mentor and partner.

Preface

I feel my stomach knot and my muscles tighten as Ben goes silent and furrows his brow. I don't want to feel this. I want to feel connected. I want to feel relaxed and benignly compassionate, knowing where I am in our conversation, and comfortably waiting for Ben to speak next. Ben has now twisted slightly in his seat and is staring at the carpet, and my body involuntarily braces, against what I'm not sure. I'm unsure what the tension is about, even as I feel it thicken.

I wrote this book because of moments like these, moments for which graduate school and post-degree training did not fully prepare me. Discussions in classrooms could not explain what it would feel like to sit in a room with someone who wanted, and at the same time did *not* want, to be there with me. I wrote this book because I know you have been here too.

There is a way my head tilts with my chin slightly up when I don't know what is happening in the therapy room. I don't know what it looks like to the patient, but I know how it feels to me. I feel like a bird: when my head tilts left my eyes stay with the patient and my right ear listens for the details of the scene my patient is speaking and the precise words she is choosing. When my head tilts to the right, I hear the music and vibrations underneath and around her words, the resonances they carry, her inflections, and the subtleties conveyed in the movement of her vocal cords, her diaphragm, her jaw, neck, and shoulders. If I don't go still like this, if instead I panic, I will feel stuck. When I panic, my hearing shuts down and I jump in—at wrong moments—trying to reassure myself that I can do something. This disrupts and scrambles my patient's message.

I want you to be unafraid to not-know what your patient will say next in similar such moments. Not-knowing in those moments is often exactly where we want to be. The place where we don't-know, and feel stuck in the therapeutic process, is often the place that holds the nub of why our patients came to see us.

In this book I want to share with you small yet important discoveries I've found along the way that moved my work forward when it felt stuck. If you are looking for grand proclamations or the theory-of-everything, you will be disappointed. "The devil's in the details," an early supervisor told me, and I have filled this book with practical details that are key to getting unstuck. You will not find formulas because each place of feeling stuck is unique. You *will* find ideas that I hope will stimulate yours. You will find clinical examples so you won't feel you are alone. You will learn about a different way of thinking, a way of relating to yourself, a way of being-with your patient, and a way of listening when you and your patient are feeling stuck.

We will look into why change that lasts takes practice and time, the power of single words to make a deep difference, and why developing a capacity for awareness may offer more bang for one's buck than a flash of insight or a causal explanation. We will explore the terrain of the worlds within—the personal snow globes in which we are each encased as we walk through life—and how change that lasts alters aspects of the architecture of those inner worlds. I will walk you through my own explorations into not-knowing and how one develops a capacity to sit in the therapy room with openness even when, or especially when, we don't know. We will examine the stuck-places that originate inside the relationship between you and your patient, and we will look bravely at the inadvertent, silent ways we are vulnerable to hurting patients if we are not aware that we are capable of doing so. Finally, we'll peer for a moment into the neglected cranny in psychotherapy of helping patients find meaning in living.

In my work I have woven together learning from several theoretical schools and from varied clinical sources such as psychological testing, psychoanalysis, hypnosis, neuroscience, working in long-term milieu hospitals, and working in brief psychotherapies. I am a pluralist. This is not an excuse; it is a commitment. My graduate program at Case Western educated us in physiology, perception, behaviorism, and research methodology, alongside psychodynamic theory, cognitive behavioral theory, and client-centered therapy. We were taught that different branches of psychological knowledge uncover different, important truths. We were instructed that research informs clinical work and vice versa. While my home theory is psychodynamic and I graduated from the Topeka Institute of Psychoanalysis, I sought diversity in my clinical training and supervision. One of my post-doctoral fellowships was in long-term therapy with adults; the other was in systems-theory approaches to children, adolescents, and families. I trained in biofeedback and EMDR, in psychological testing and neuropsychological testing. I spent 30 years training, teaching and becoming board-certified in clinically applied hypnosis. Cross-disciplinary fertilization is the science of the future. This holds true in mental health, where there need not be a king theory and its subordinates, but rather equal countries that learn from each other and pool their wisdom.

Ben and I went dozens more times into his stormy place of swelling tension. Each time we learned more about what that place was and what Ben was trying to say inside it. With my help holding the rudder steady on our partnering through those rough seas, Ben learned to harness the power inside his tension. That didn't happen because I understood what the tension meant. It happened because I allowed myself to not understand. We found our way because I quieted the noises of blame inside my head and focused on riding the waves of uncertainty. I slowed my reactivity down and opened my receptivity to what was there to be discovered inside our shared tension.

You may be a psychodynamic therapist or a cognitive-behavioral one. You may be a social worker in a family-focused clinic or a psychiatrist who primarily dispenses medication and who wants to connect more with your patients. You may have just received your degree or, like me, you may have practiced for enough decades to encounter situations for which your theory-base did not fully prepare you. What joins all of us is we want to help people and we know that we sometimes don't know how. I hope I can inspire in you the wonder inside this place of feeling stuck and not-knowing. It is a gift we are given to be able to learn something new. It is a sacred trust we hold when we invite our patient to share themselves with us. I want you to feel less of the fear and more of the wonder and sacred trust when you feel tense or confused. I want you to come to appreciate that if we listen, the knowing will come.

1 Change Takes Time

We soon learn that achieving substantial change is not easy.

(Schlesinger, 1976, p. 1)

A person walking into a psychotherapist's office for the first time wants to feel better when she walks out. We want her to feel better too. But how is her sensation of feeling "better" related to change?

To feel better, connection is essential. Our patient needs to feel this stranger, her potential therapist, grasps something about who she really is and what she is trying to say. There needs to be a "click."

The therapist's competence is in play as well. Our patient needs to feel the person she is entrusting herself to has experience with what she brings and will be able to help her.

Connection combined with competence sparks hope. But maybe our patient can't trust hope yet because hope has let her down too often. In this case, can she feel intrigued by the way her therapist frames something, or how he pauses to think when she thought there was nothing there to think about? Hope and curiosity are fuel for the work of change.

I said the "work" of change because change is different from feeling better. It does not have to be grueling work (though occasionally it might feel that way), but it does take intention and time.

Learning Braille

Let's look at what happens when the brain learns so that we might understand this bond between change and time. We know the brain has plasticity, meaning it reconfigures itself structurally in order to tackle new challenges and adapt to new information. But for those reconfigurations to stick and become *change* rather than momentary adjustments, one must put in repetitions over time.

Doidge (2007) describes a study by Alvaro Pascual-Leone in which people who were learning Braille allowed their brains to be mapped with Transcranial Magnetic Stimulation (TMS). The students worked on Braille

DOI: 10.4324/9781315449043-1

three hours daily (one hour of class plus two hours of study) Monday through Friday. They underwent TMS every Monday and Friday. After a week of study, on Friday, TMS showed their brains had changed structurally, reflecting the effects of their learning ("Friday maps"). By Monday, however, after a weekend of no studying, the changes seen on Friday had evaporated ("Monday maps"). The discovery that brain changes didn't stick despite diligently applying oneself to learning is not encouraging news for teachers, students, or psychotherapists. Thankfully, that was not the end of the story. When subjects persisted at their learning schedule *every week, across six months* (390 hours), the TMS brain mapping showed the Friday maps holding through the weekend into Monday. No longer were the structural reconfigurations slipping away; the Monday maps showed the changes were sticking. There is more: after an additional four months of Braille-work (ten months total; 650 hours of direct work), the changes seen in the brain remained stable even across two months of no practicing (Doidge, 2007, pp. 198–199).

Two Kinds of Change

We are always changing. Change is the unstoppable product of the life force within us. The epidermal layer of our skin replaces itself every four weeks. The same happens with the lining of our intestines over about five days. Edelman and Tononi (2000) describe that even consciousness is *continuously* transmuting. Flow patterns of neural messaging fluidly reconfigure millisecond by millisecond in response to incoming data. One could imagine the "shape" of our consciousness—i.e., the constellations formed from the patterns of synaptic firings—being a constantly undulating light-show as information registers across and absorbs into our neural net. It is as if we are constantly getting chances at do-overs.

We are, even if we don't realize it. The type of change I just described is the energy of continuous adaptation. We change spontaneously in this way until we die. Who knows? Change may continue to happen in some form after our bodies shut down.

Spontaneous adaptational change is not the same as intentional change, change that we choose. In psychotherapy, we are looking to harness the natural energy of adaptational change, and to do so *intentionally*, in order to consciously reshape the trajectory of our patient's growth in a new direction. We want her change to last. We want that fist-pumping, Friday-map achievement to prevail over the weekend into Monday, and beyond.

Change That Lasts

Jean Piaget understood the distinction between momentary adjustments and change that results in transformation. Nearly a century ago he spent thousands of hours observing children as they grappled with confusing aspects of the world: for example, how the amount of water poured into a short fat beaker could be the same amount that was in a tall thin beaker, when the water level was clearly higher in the taller beaker. Piaget asked the children questions about how they were reasoning through the puzzles he gave them to solve and using their answers traced a path along which cognitive constructs evolve into greater sophistication. Two mileposts along that path are Assimilation and Accommodation (Piaget, 1952). Assimilation is absorbing experiences into mental constructs that already exist. Accommodation occurs when existing constructs can no longer hold and explain what is taking place and new paradigms are forced into existence. New constructs are created only when experience repeatedly disproves a person's old assumptions.

Behaviorists understood the difference between the two kinds of change in the early 20th century when they experimented with the conditioning and extinction of behavior. They constructed a mathematical scaffolding for change that lasts, a structure of equations for the number of repetitions of reinforcement and absence of reinforcement required before new behavior locked in or old behavior dissipated (Hull, 1943; Pavlov, 1927; Skinner, 1938; Watson, 1925).

Susan Vaughan (1997) understood the distinction as well. Vaughan was both a psychoanalyst and a student of the neuroscientist Eric Kandel. She instinctively understood the relationship between talking, feeling, and relating in psychotherapy and changes in the cellular structure and chemistry of the brain. Freud's free associations of thoughts were synchronously envisioned by her as synaptic pathways. As Vaughan (1997) said:

> It takes repeated pairings...Just as random exercises at the gym will not necessarily build or reshape one particular muscle, chance meanderings in your neural networks are unlikely to sculpt a particular part of your brain. Getting a trainer and learning his or her strategies for accomplishing your goal is a good first step toward change, but change nevertheless requires time and the repetition of the useful exercises. (p. 71)

Change that is more than a momentary adjustment is a physiological revision. This is the kind of change our patient is seeking when she arrives. To be able to speak clearly in a business meeting instead of being stricken mute by anxiety, she needs more than ideas and explanations. She needs altered biological processes and structures. This means: networks of neuronal messaging rerouting; brain areas redistributing their volume; chemical response-sequences rearranging; perception shifting its figure-ground prioritizations. This is the stuff of transformation. One patient described it as if she had broken through into a different world, like the character Truman near the end of the movie, *The Truman Show*.

Physiological revision not only lasts; it sets the patient on a new developmental trajectory going forward. As Appelbaum (1977) observed in his research: "Psychotherapy sets a process in motion which continues even when the treatment per se is ended" (p 268).

The quandary is that the patient arriving for her first session, the one who is intuitively seeking for her Monday-maps to change, is also likely, given our culture, expecting this change to happen fast. Waiting five days for a package to arrive is considered unacceptable. Waiting for an outgoing phone greeting to end before being able to leave a voicemail can be agitating. Waiting 15 seconds for a website to load feels slow. Fast has become synonymous with sharper, smarter, better; we are even encouraged to *fail* fast. The reality is that we are not AI. We may register instantaneously; we may be able to comprehend instantaneously if we're not grappling with something new, but we cannot *change* instantaneously. We don't suddenly sprout new paradigms or pave new neural pathways from hearing or reading something once. Change that lasts beyond a momentary startle and beyond the end of therapy takes intentional, focused repetition over time.

Aligning Our Patient's Expectations

Psychotherapy can feel stuck for our patient if the time it is taking for her to feel different begins to diverge from how long she thought it would take. "Would" turns into "should" and our patient's discouragement turns into concern that the psychotherapy is not working. If we explore our patient's expectations from the beginning we can avoid this confusion. We don't want to mislead her into expecting it will take less time than it will. On the other hand, we don't want to misrepresent the process as having to take years.

The fact that change takes repetition does *not* mean that psychotherapy takes forever. Sawing through a two-inch branch—repeatedly moving our arm back and forth—takes time. That two-inch branch takes fewer sawing repetitions and less time to cut through than a five-inch log does. The estimated length of the psychotherapy depends on what we and our patient choose to accomplish.

The time psychotherapy takes also depends on the energy and practice the patient is willing to put in, both inside and outside the sessions. Pascual-Leone's study did not examine how long it took for brain changes to stick in subjects who participated in one-hour daily Braille classes without studying for the two hours afterwards. But we do know, without having to look at brain maps, that the more hours a person practices a piano between lessons the more adroit her fingers become. The more time a person spends on physical therapy exercises, the faster her muscles strengthen and her range of motion increases. The same is true for the emotional work of psychotherapy.

Empathizing With Patients' Time Pressures and Time Needs

When we discuss time with our patient, we need to take at face value any concerns she has about how little free time there is in her life. We shouldn't automatically take her worries as signals that she is ambivalent about therapy or has trouble with commitment. As I write this book, the median home value in the United States doubled between 1960 and 2000 when we correct for inflation (Historical census of housing tables, home values, n.d.). During that same time period, family income of the bottom 60% of our population flatlined (Mislinski, 2018). The percentage of families with two working spouses accordingly rose by 50% and the percentage of mothers who were breadwinners rose by 130% (Dionne, 2012; Glynn, 2012). More people need to work more hours just to stay even, and staying even no longer means being able to afford the same perks their money used to buy. People and families are time-starved.

The digital technology explosion squeezes time as well. We are expected to know more and know it more quickly in order to keep pace with competing peers and job demands. We are expected to be available by phone, text, and laptop during what used to be considered downtime. People telework from airports, take conference calls while driving kids to school, and awaken at 3 am to network with colleagues in Tokyo. Who has time for psychotherapy?

Making such pressures discussable and normal helps patients feel understood. Psychotherapy is a luxury, even when it is a necessity. "Why should I choose to spend my (very limited) time on this?" is a reasonable question. Addressing our patient's concern is one of our first experiments in partnering. If we understand how to look "under the hood" at what is driving her symptoms rather than assigning her complaints mechanically to predetermined interventions, we will be able to answer her question cogently. We will be equipped to present options with time estimates and the relative pros and cons of each. Staying with the car metaphor, our patient may not need an engine overhaul; she may just need a new fan belt. On the other hand, if she needs an engine overhaul we want to be able to describe to her in accurate, clear language why this is in her best interests (Peebles, 2012; Peebles-Kleiger, 2002).

Step by Step

Change that lasts is incremental. We build psychological capacities in steps, in the same way a seed unfolds underground, emerges, and eventually blossoms, or a two month old lays the foundation for walking when she pushes up from her stomach to raise her head. Growth is sequences of tiny shifts filling in patterns laid out for us in the biology of human development (Greenspan, 1997). This is true in psychotherapy whether we meet for a few sessions or a few years. It is true, whether we work on a straightforward fear of flying or more complicated matters such as refining the handling of emotions, altering entrenched character structure, or resolving trauma (Peebles, 2012). If we understand the developmental steps for different psychological capacities, we can speak to our patient about pieces of work.

Swimming with Time, Rather than Fighting It

Pieces of Work

We don't need to be over-zealous as therapists. Not everything that could be tackled in psychotherapy needs to be tackled in *this* therapy episode. If the work bogs down, it helps to reflect back on our initial assessment, which ideally included identifying pieces of work for the patient and offering pluses and minuses for if and when to do each. Perhaps we have veered away from our original goals. Maybe we slid without thinking into a new piece of work. Are we pushing for too much growth? Would it be wiser to sit back with our patient and help her appreciate what she has accomplished already? We know that efficacy in one area will stimulate efficacy in other areas naturally because efficacy invigorates capacities and belief. A psychotherapy job well done is one that helps the patient back onto a healthy trajectory of growth, from which point she can continue developing on her own. Thinking in terms of pieces of work allows us to work as briefly as possible and as deeply as necessary to make this possible.

As we adopt a pieces-of-work mindset, we are better able to recognize movement in our patient's growth and point it out to her, whether we are working from a behavioral, dynamic, cognitive, humanistic, systemic or biological point of view. Identifying progress sharpens the work's focus; it makes the time spent feel productive rather than stagnant. It builds persistence because it builds an experience of competence for the patient, which engenders hope. Rats who were given brief interludes of rest atop a dry platform, kept swimming in a barrel of water for days on end simply because they had learned that the possibility of dryness existed (Menninger et al., 1963; Richter, 1957. Teaching our patient to recognize incremental progress extends to her the gift of *experiencing* her own mastery. Mastery is an invaluable byproduct of psychotherapy. It infuses us with self-respect, and self-respect is a sturdy foundation internally, sturdy enough to shoulder hope through reversals and disappointment.

Frequency

Decisions about frequency of psychotherapy sessions are sometimes reached arbitrarily, without understanding the myths about frequency and the actual ways in which frequency shapes the therapeutic process. Patients often believe that more frequent meetings mean they have more severe illness and infrequent sessions means they're healthier. As a result, their stomachs knot if we suggest that meeting twice a week would be useful. Similarly, sometimes therapists are unsure what benefit higher or lower frequency provides. They may agree with a time-pressured patient to once monthly sessions out of respect for her limited time resources, not realizing that meeting less frequently might actually mean the therapy will take longer and may not even accomplish what she is looking for.

How frequently we meet with a patient is governed by what goals we are trying to attain, what parameters will help her get there, and what she can manage emotionally. The less frequently we meet, the more likely it is that the session's time will be used reporting events that occurred since the prior session. Such a situation may be a good fit for a patient who is maintaining growth that she has already achieved working with us. We know her well; she is likely stable; and monthly sessions may be a perfect match for checking in and refreshing concepts for her that may have slipped from mind. On the other hand, if we are trying to get to know a new patient, to help new ideas and experience gain traction, or we need loose time in sessions for discovery, reflection, and discussion, then once-monthly frequency is going to be inadequate.

Frequency also needs to be tied to what a patient can manage emotionally. More frequent meetings intensifies the interpersonal process. This is true for any relationship, including psychotherapy. Because there is more time and smaller gaps between meetings, there is more we learn and feel about each other, more room for those emotions and perceptions to bloom, and more opportunities for trust, distrust, disclosure, or friction to develop. We must assess to what degree and under what conditions we and our patient can manage intensification of the experience without her destabilizing or her symptoms being exacerbated. How equipped are we to manage the situation clinically if she worsens? Do we have sufficient training? Can we be accessed easily after hours? Do we have a network of colleagues to whom we could turn for consultation or assistance in hospitalization? These concerns need to be considered.

On the other hand, some patients hold on to a close experience with us longer than benefits them because they trust us and feel nourished by the healthy communication with us. At the right point, they may need a gentle nudge away from the comforting familiarity of therapy and into the outer world to put their skills into practice and grow equally nourishing relationships there. For these patients, meeting once every two weeks may be just what they need to stretch their autonomy, feel their competence for cultivating emotionally enriching opportunities, and talk with us about what they encounter when they do.

Still other patients have difficulty maintaining trust in us between sessions because without direct, sensory feedback of who we actually are, their minds fill with memories of how others acted toward them: people who were exploitative, derisive, or unconcerned. In this situation, greater frequency of sessions stabilizes the work.

Decisions about frequency require knowledge and sensitivity. Frequency is like the soundtrack in a movie. It moves the story forward in unique, nuanced ways if chosen wisely.

Juncture-Moments; Juncture-Sessions

Taking a read on what the patient needs, what has been accomplished thus far, and what more needs to take place is an ongoing calibration. Juncture-moments are those intentional pauses that we insert into a session, in which we notice and share with the patient evidence of her growth, comparing how she just responded with how she responded to a similar dilemma weeks or months earlier. A juncture-moment expands hope and mastery. It also organizes and focuses loose strands of work by connecting them for our patient to her original symptoms and our original shared goals. This allows our patient to see where she is along the path. For example, I might say, "I'm noticing as we were talking the last ten minutes how you were able to listen, and absorb what I was saying, without flinching and pushing it away out of shame. You were curious and interested. This is very different from just ten months ago. You're not assuming automatically that I'm putting you down. Something has shifted. You're experiencing yourself as someone of value, rather than that pervasive 'trash' feeling you described when you first came to see me." When we do this regularly, patients internalize juncture-moments as a way of thinking. They begin noticing incremental growth in their day-to-day living.

There are also juncture-sessions. These are particularly important when the work has been hard and questions have arisen about its usefulness, either from the patient or in our own mind. I offer the idea collaboratively to my patient, suggesting that we use a session specifically to take stock of our work thus far. "It might be helpful just to look back on where we started, why you came to see me and what you hoped I could help you with. We can go over what you feel has changed, where you may feel disappointed, and where you'd like to go from here." Juncture-sessions save time by tightening the focus for meandering work and by identifying possible causes for stalled work. They underscore choice. In these sessions we invite our patient to renew their partnership with us, and we do so with respect for their autonomy and point of view. Juncture-sessions are an opportunity to commit to an updated treatment plan rather than be carried along by a process that has lost its definition.

A Psychological IRA

The time we spend in therapy is an investment in our emotional future; I frequently refer to psychotherapy as a psychological IRA (individual retirement account). Each healthy choice we learn to make as a result of therapy leads to healthier relationships and self-expression. Self-worth grows, agency strengthens, and subsequent choices become wiser. In this way, our investment of time compounds over time.

Psychotherapy strengthens one's emotional resilience in the face of adversity. As people age, external gratifications such as purchases, travel, sports, glitz, and hubbub, which once offset internal distress, become less accessible. Personal talents that may have once smoothed a balm over us of feeling relevant and sought after wane as well. There are relational loses, losses of physical capacities, and losses of the familiar. Children grow and leave home; parents and friends die; neighborhoods change; we downsize our homes. Psychotherapy grows a sense of value and contentment that we can generate internally. Our well-being becomes less dependent on external circumstances over which we have lessening control.

For a young adult with long horizons, the appeal of psychotherapy-as-investment increases. Untangling one's sources of distress and distorted perceptions improves choices about life-satisfaction-determining matters such as partners and careers (Yapko, 2009). If mistakes are our teachers, in the long run it feels better to learn from those teachers early, so we avoid the frustrations and losses incurred from having to be schooled by the same lessons over and over again.

Altering the course of an airplane a mere four degrees as it travels from London to New York City will shift the nose of the plane from the skyscrapers of Manhattan to the Finger Lakes Forests of Vermont. Adjustments to our "flight plan" through engaging in psychotherapy can shift our life course in exponential ways.

Feeling Stuck is Not Always a Bad Thing

Feeling stuck in psychotherapy is actually *the* place of opportunity. Stuck is where our patient has been living before she met us, or else she would not have made her first appointment. The difference is this time she and we are arriving at her place of stuck together. Feeling stuck is not a welcome sensation. It makes us uneasy and tests our confidence, yet it is an invaluable vantage point. Our *involvement* in our patient's stuck place allows us to feel sensations that would be difficult for her name, and to notice interpersonal sequences that are near-impossible to catch when they occur in one's own life. Such information is accessible only through live engagement and allows us to pinpoint the very moment that our patient's interactions, thoughts, or perceptions clog.

Feeling stuck is not always a conscious sensation. Sometimes it descends on us like fog. We have a hard time following what our patient is saying. We feel tired; we think we are bored. Sometimes we misread the sensation of being stuck and conclude it is time to finish therapy, that the patient has gone as far as she can go. Maybe we look forward to her canceling or to her showing up late. Sometimes it is the patient who senses it first and shows it by being testy with us, not wanting to complain or not even knowing what to complain about. Sometimes she cancels sessions for reasons that on the surface seem perfectly reasonable but the cancellations begin to occur more frequently. Or she runs out of things to say and says her mind feels blank. Classical psychoanalysis used to call these actions "resistance," believing the patient was throwing obstacles in the path of progress. That isn't quite it and it certainly isn't always the case. Sometimes she and we are stuck, and we just don't know it yet.

It helps to be sensitive to such subtle experiences and consider "feeling stuck" as a possible cause. We name this possibility to ourselves and then aloud to our patient. We speak in a spirit of curiosity, not judgment. We want to convey interest and a "we," not shaming or chastisement of "them." I had a patient who jumped in and said, "Oh—you mean I'm showing resistance." "No," I said. "I don't experience you as wanting to feel worse or trying to make this not work. I'm wondering instead what you might be trying to express that I'm not picking up, and my not hearing you is leaving us adrift just as you said happened in your family." Tagging a moment in this way can be a significant step toward becoming unstuck because often our patient has never had anyone willing to be stuck with her, much less interested in staying there alongside her and figuring it out together as a team.

Chapter Two takes us into the sensory music of words. How we speak to our patient is the heartbeat of interventions. Sometimes it is the words we choose that unwittingly keep a process stuck.

References

Appelbaum, S.A. (1977). *The anatomy of change*. New York, NY: Plenum Press.

Dionne, E.J. (2012, April 18). Two-paycheck couples are quickly becoming the norm. *Washington Post*: Opinion. https://www.washingtonpost.com/opinions/two-paycheck-couples-are-quickly-becoming-the-norm/2012/04/18/gIQALSzlRT_story.html?noredirect=on

Doidge, N. (2007). *The brain that changes itself: Stories of personal triumph from the frontiers of brain science*. New York, NY: Penguin Books.

Edelman, G.M., & Tononi, G. (2000). *A universe of consciousness: How matter becomes imagination*. New York, NY: Basic Books.

Glynn, S.J. (2012, April 16). The new breadwinners: 2012 update. *Center for American Progress, Economy*. https://www.americanprogress.org/issues/economy/reports/2012/04/16/11377/the-new-breadwinners-2010-update/

Greenspan, S.I. (1997). *Developmentally based psychotherapy*. Madison, CT: International Universities Press.

Historical census of housing tables, home values (n.d.). United States Census Bureau. https://www.census.gov/hhes/www/housing/census/historic/values.html

Hull, C.L. (1943). *Principles of behavior*. New York, NY: Appleton-Century-Crofts.

Menninger, C.F., Mayman, M., & Pruyser, P. (1963). *The vital balance: The life process in mental health and illness*. New York, NY: The Viking Press.

Mislinski, J. (2018, October 16). U.S. household incomes: A 51-year perspective. https://www.advisorperspectives.com/dshort/updates/2018/10/16/u-s-household-incomes-a-51-year-perspective

Pavlov, I.P. (1927). *Conditioned reflexes* (G.V. Anrep, trans.). London, UK: Oxford University Press.

Peebles, M.J. (2012). *Beginnings: The art and science of planning psychotherapy* (2nd ed.). New York, NY: Routledge Press.

Peebles-Kleiger, M.J. (2002). *The art and science of planning psychotherapy*. Hillsdale, NJ: The Analytic Press.

Piaget, J. (1952). *The origins of intelligence in children* (M. Cook, trans.). New York, NY: International Universities Press.

Richter, C.P. (1957), The phenomenon of unexplained sudden death in animals and man. In H. Feifel (Ed.), *The meaning of death* (pp. 302–313). New York, NY: McGraw-Hill.

Schlesinger, H.J. (1976, October 28). *The responsibility of the psychoanalyst for analytic and therapeutic change* [Paper presentation]. Topeka Psychoanalytic Society Meeting, The Menninger Clinic, Topeka, KS.

Skinner, B.F. (1938). *The behavior of organisms: An experimental analysis*. New York, NY: Appleton-Century-Crofts.

Vaughan, S.C. (1997). *The talking cure: Why traditional talking therapy offers a better chance for long-term relief than any drug*. New York, NY: Henry Holt and Company.

Watson, J.B. (1925). *Behaviorism*. New York, NY: W.W. Norton.

Yapko, M. (2009). *Depression is contagious: How the most common mood disorder is spreading around the world and how we can stop it*. New York, NY: Free Press, Simon & Schuster, Inc.

2 How We Say It Matters

What we say, what we omit, and how we say it matters very much.
—Dabney Ewin, *101 Things I Wish I'd Known When I Started Using Hypnosis*

Psychotherapy can become stuck when what we say does not match what we want to happen. By "we," I mean therapists and patients alike. Let's start with Becky.

My

Becky had pored over glossy travel brochures since she was twelve. Two and a half decades later, she was now traveling to places she had once only dreamed about. Planning her journeys—whether to Iceland, Turkey, or Vietnam—made her days fly by and her world fill with possibility. As I watched her eyes sparkle describing the beauty of an Asian village, I puzzled how this fearless explorer could suffer gut-clenching anxiety.

"I saw my first therapist in Middle School. I was waking up with dread inside—*every morning*—and when I got to school I shook. It felt like the walls were closing in on me. This lasted almost a year. My mom told me that I'd be fine, that it was just hard to start 6th grade. But then it wasn't fine, and when it didn't go away my mom found a therapist for me. I remember the therapist said I had 'social anxiety.' I was relieved there was a name for it, because a name meant I wasn't crazy. I'm pretty sure my anxiety is inherited from my mother. In high school and college, I thought I was managing it ok. I would remember things my therapist told me about not over-generalizing. And that would help, and when it didn't, I'd take a Xanax to get through a really bad day. But now my anxiety isn't going away. I'm having trouble sleeping. I'm afraid of how it's coming back. It's a horrible feeling. I understand my anxiety is a

DOI: 10.4324/9781315449043-2

lifelong illness, but I want to get on top of it somehow—so it doesn't get as bad as it was before. That's why I came here—I thought maybe if I had a few sessions, I could build up my skills, like I did before."

A patient's attitude toward her pain shapes her reality and determines what will or will not change in psychotherapy. Her relationship with her suffering is revealed in how she speaks.

When a patient uses "my" to describe feelings of depression or anxiety, as Becky did above, she is letting us know about possessiveness. Each time she uses "my," she glues her condition onto herself more firmly. She is telling us that her depression or anxiety "belongs" to her; it is a part of her.

There are many reasons people hold tight to their conditions. Sometimes a person has tried multiple treatments and nothing has worked. Caregivers may have told her she suffers from an "intractable" illness, or a medical professional may have named her disorder and it became the only name she learned to use.

A person's illness may have solved something important. For example, an adolescent being given a diagnosis of depression might have stopped her father from yelling at her and brought the parents together to protect her.

A person may have lived so long with a condition, or it entered her life during formative years, that the *condition* became indistinguishable from identity.

Whatever the reasons for "my," the implications for psychotherapy are similar: the patient and her illness have a special relationship. They have been companions long before patient and psychotherapist met. For change to occur, we must loosen "my's" adhesiveness, and explore the space left when the patient loses certainty that her depression or anxiety will always be with her.

To work with "my," we must listen with engagement.

Listening with engagement means we experience who our patient is *being*, not merely who she is describing herself to be. We are interested and curious, not detached or silently examining. We share what we observe. We can always be frank if we are respectful and kind.

Listening with engagement also means we ask our patient's help in understanding what is not yet making sense to us. If we assume that a skilled therapist would be able to understand why someone suddenly cries, erupts, or blinks in confusion, we are pressuring ourselves needlessly. The truth is there is no way we can know. We can guess, but asking our patient to help us is putting two good minds together on the same task. Our patient grows from such moments. She learns that someone is not afraid to not have all the answers. She learns that she is necessary to the partnership. She learns that someone *wants* to hear what is inside her. She learns that she can think and speak even as she is feeling. She experiences a person wanting to learn who she is, rather than telling her who she is.

As I listened to Becky, I watched the different movements of her body—across her face and in her eyes. I felt the fluctuations in her tone and rhythm. I could see and hear that despite her use of "my," Becky was not continuously anxious. Sometimes she joked, laughed freely, or relaxed. Sometimes she became still, and her eyes softened as she absorbed my words. Now and then, she tightened up and her words would stumble rather than flow, but those anxious moments were not the bulk of what occurred. Becky's description of herself did not match who she was being with me.

As I continued to ask Becky questions about her experience rather than assuming I understood, her anxious moments dwindled. I noticed a pattern: when I spoke something that Becky felt captured what she'd been struggling to explain, the tension in her shoulders and face relaxed, her eyes watered, and her throat choked a small sob. Becky was startled when this happened. She wasn't used to the feeling.

I asked for her help. "I see emotion in your face...what is it saying?"

Becky looked as if she were feeling and thinking, trying to work out the right words. "This thing [the experience she'd just been trying to describe] has not been describable before. I just feel like, relief—to be speaking all this. You get what I'm trying to say. Those words [you used] are exactly right. I don't know...it's almost as if this is something I've been looking for, for a long time." She began openly crying. "I feel relief and new ideas already."

I stretched her. "Where is the feeling of anxiety right now, as you are telling me this?"

Becky looked surprised. Hesitantly, she said, "I feel...calmer...I'm not feeling the anxiety."

Perhaps your ears just noticed what mine did: in that moment, "my" became "the" for Becky. A bit of glue loosened. In addition, we gained information about the tension Becky had been calling "my anxiety." She had been holding in, for too long and too alone, feelings and thoughts that she didn't know how to share or word. Becky remembered being told, "Don't think about it," when she expressed upset as a little girl. Because no one had asked, she had not learned how to speak her sensory experience of life. Becky had been searching for someone to engage with her on the inside, but hadn't known how to ask for that.

What happened for Becky during that first session was not magic. It merely shows what can unfold when we don't assume we know what a person means, and when we pay attention to *how* a person is saying something, not just what he is saying.

In the beginning, Becky could not trust my idea that she might not have a lifelong illness. I needed to guide her to the data I was taking in, to notice and track her own physical sensations. By doing so, she began to catch the variations in her feelings of tension. She began to appreciate how those variations were offering valuable information rather than being random attacks of an ungovernable illness. Over time, Becky's relationship with anxiety changed. Anxiety became a signal for her to slow down and listen carefully for what she was registering but not yet wording. It is a lovely postscript that Becky eventually began publishing poetry with deeply sensory images of experiences that once she could not speak.

The Power of a Word

There is so much power in words that we do not want to rob ourselves of their effectiveness as interventions. Words determine how we think, perceive, and proceed. The words therapists think determine their optimism about the work, their emotional experience of patients, and ultimately their tipping point for burnout. The words patients use shape their assumptions about how much agency they can have over their lives and whether or not something different is possible.

A single word activates complex webs of associational networks in tenths of milliseconds (Edelman & Tononi, 2000).

Daniel Kahneman (2011) breaks down research demonstrating how word-choices, and the subliminal reverberations they activate, drive decision-making more than facts do. He says, "The reason [people] don't change their mind is...that facts don't matter, or they matter *much* less than people think" (Tippett, 2017; 50:55 to 51:19). Westen (2007) illustrates the same point in politics. Elections turn on choices of words and pictures. "The choice of words, images, sounds, music, backdrop, tone of voice, and a host of other factors is likely to be as significant to the electoral success of a campaign as its content" (Westen, 2007, p. 87).

Linguists walk us through the specifics (Boroditsky, 2011). For example, using an active, transitive verb heightens perceptions of blame. 589 people read a prepared description of Janet Jackson's 2004 Super Bowl "wardrobe malfunction." Half the group read a description with the active voice of agentive language ("...he [Justin Timberlake] unfastened a snap and tore part of [Janet Jackson's] bodice! He slid the cover right off Jackson's chest!" [Fausey & Boroditsky, 2010, p. 648]). Half read a description written with the passive voice of non-agentive language ("...a snap unfastened and part of [Janet Jackson's] bodice tore! The cover slid right off Jackson's chest!" [p. 648]). Those who read the passive, intransitive verbs were less likely to blame Timberlake for Jackson's exposure and assigned 53% less financial liability to him, even after they watched the actual video footage. This is remarkable: a shift in syntax influenced not only what people thought, but what they saw. (Here is what I saw when I watched the footage: Janet Jackson stopped at the front of the stage facing the crowd with her feet planted about two feet apart. Her chin and eyes tilted down toward the left. Timberlake approached on her left. He stopped, angled 45 degrees to Jackson, in an open stance toward the crowd. His body was against hers. His right hand held a microphone and was positioned behind Jackson's body, just to the right of her left shoulder blade. During the next 1.5 to 2 seconds, the following happened. Timberlake's left hand flattened against Jackson's left abdomen palm down. Jackson stopped swaying. Timberlake reached his left hand across Jackson's chest. His fingers curled around something just under Jackson's right armpit. Then he pulled in one long continuous movement away from her chest leftward across her body and across his body, carrying a black piece of fabric in his hand as he did so.)

Eyes scan scenes according to how those scenes are described. When listeners hear, "The fence follows the coastline," (Richardson & Matlock, 2007, p. 130), they spend more time gazing at a picture of a fence and coastline, and they *move their eyes across* the picture, as if literally following a fence that is moving. In contrast, if listeners hear, "The fence is next to the coastline," (p. 131), their eyes scarcely move, and they spend little time looking. Their static gaze mirrors the static description.

Transitive vs. intransitive verbs cause us to remember differently. If we prime a person's mind with passive-tense verbs having no agency (e.g., "The shirt shrunk." "The grill ignited."), the person is less likely to remember agency (who did what) in a subsequent video. In contrast, people primed with agency-filled transitive verbs (e.g., "He shrunk the shirt." "He ignited the grill.") are better able to remember who performed actions in a subsequent video (Fausey et al., 2010). Hearing agency in something as subtle as verb form influences people's ability to see and remember agency.

Single words can alter opinions and actions (Thibodeau et al., 2017). When cancer is described as an "enemy" rather than a neutral force, people more actively restrain themselves and become preventative (e.g., eat less red meat, drink less alcohol). When a loving relationship is described as a "journey" rather than a "perfect union," conflict in that relationship hurts less. When crime is described as a "virus," support for social reform rises; when it is described as a "beast," support for law enforcement rises.

The way words are delivered can scramble the mind. Bateson et al. (1956) analyzed tapes of interviews and spontaneous interactions with patients with schizophrenic illness and their parents. From this data, Bateson et al. coined the term "double-bind" communication. Double-bind communication occurs when the literal message spoken contradicts the subtextual message communicated in word-choice, tone, phrasing, and inflection. For example, if a mother responds to a child's anger with, "You don't mean that," spoken in a soothing tone, *and* inflected with a threatening imperative, the child is in a bind. Should he organize his reality around what *he* spoke—that he is angry? Or should he organize around what mother spoke—that he is not angry? Should he pay attention to mother's soothing tone? Or should he become vigilant given mother's menacing inflection? Any response he gives effaces some part of the reality he is perceiving. No response feels safe. When a child grows up in a family with double-bind communication, he may not develop schizophrenic illness; however, his mental processing will show damage years later. Even if he is highly intelligent, he will feel compelled to rethink his interpersonal perceptions many times over. Even if he is articulate, he will be afraid to speak his true feelings clearly. He will obfuscate his meaning—even to himself—through a tangle of qualifiers, evasions, and retractions in order to avoid being caught saying something "unallowable."

How we speak matters.

Verb Tense Places Us in Time

When people grow, it takes time for their inner experience of who they are to catch up with the changes they have made. A classic example of this is when a person slims down by 80 pounds but still feels as if he inhabits his old, heavier body. When the gap between an old sense of Self and new behavior does not close, growth stalls. Patients need our help to close such gaps.

A person's subjective experience of "this is who I am" is shaped by reflections from others. This point was brought home in Sartre's play, *No Exit*, in which Hell is depicted as three people locked inside rooms with no mirrors, and only each other's warped perceptions from which to derive a sense of who they are. Therapy must stand as the antithesis to Sartre's *No Exit*. We therapists train and undergo personal therapy in order to see our patients as clearly as possible, without emotional distortions. When we offer objective reflections to a patient, we help him inhabit, in a sensory way, the person he has become. When our patient feels his newly developing Self physically in his body and not just as an idea, he can retrieve this feeling and rehearse it until it consolidates fully.

The verb tense a patient uses signals whether or not he has subjectively caught up with the changes he has made. The verb tense we respond with telegraphs back to him where we objectively see him to be. When we consciously attend to verb tense in this way, we help a patient consolidate his changes.

Andrea's situation illustrates this idea.

Andrea was an executive at a start-up company. Her self-value was derived from performing impeccably. Whether as an attacker in high school lacrosse, a team member in business school, or as the lead on a work project, Andrea dedicated herself to the goal until the win was clinched.

As Andrea's life became more complex, her former winning solution of being alert to tiny details, tagging all that fell short of expectations, and clocking the time it would take to fix problems was no longer working. There simply was not enough time. Andrea, however, clung to her old approach; she was convinced it was the only path to victory over mounting demands. I stepped aside from her invitation to argue her point of view; instead, I suggested she expand her nimble scanning of details to include what was going right.

Andrea could not resist a challenge and quickly tackled this one. Eventually, I asked her to notice how her body felt whenever she discovered something working well. For example, when she saw her kitchen countertop cleared of clutter, what sensations did she become aware of? When her daughter nestled her head into the crook of Andrea's arm, how did that feel? I was re-channeling Andrea's natural inclinations; noticing details was harnessed for tracking what was going right. Focus was channeled into capturing soothing sensations. Her passion for organizing and prioritizing was introduced to the efficiency gained from taking one-step-at-a-time, restoring stamina, and valuing "good-enough."

One afternoon, during a tension-filled visit with her in-laws, Andrea and her husband Jon escaped by jumping into their parents' pool and floating to the middle together. The sun was sharp, the water blue, and her husband held her. For a moment—probably no longer than 90 seconds—all seemed at peace as they dangled in the water, weightless, simply staring at the sparkling blue of the sky, and feeling the skin-upon-skin touch of each other's arms.

I commented quietly, "How different that was. The way noise faded, and space stretched out, and you and Jon just floated. ...Timelessly."

"But then it ended!" Andrea protested, her mind reflexively drawn to what went wrong.

"Yes... True. And.... it was also there—the entire time," I mused, balancing her back into what went right. "And.... it was *you* who made it happen—the floating. You *allowed* it. You *felt* it. You *lingered* in it." I stretched the word linger out long, like taffy, to stretch out the time in which Andrea might absorb its significance.

"You're right!" she said as if checking off a to-do list. "I need to be able to feel the good things and let them last! I need to learn how to do that, like you're saying, to allow it to happen!" Notice how Andrea was using the future tense.

"You're *already doing* it," I smiled, holding her gaze with steady eyes. "In the pool...the floating with Jon. *That's exactly what it feels like*. It is no longer something you have to 'start' doing. You're already doing it." Notice how I countered with the present progressive tense.

A light clicked on in Andrea's eyes. The shift in verb tense had shifted her consciousness. From being stuck inside who she had been, she momentarily dislodged, and flicked into a present tense experience of who she had become.

Try

Try is a misleading word. While it is a promise that conveys earnest effort, it implies never quite reaching what it is striving toward. Try's energy dissipates itself inside the limbo of *almost*.

The subconscious mind recognizes try's ambiguities. As Dabney Ewin (2009) put it, "The word [try] implies failure. I only use it when I *don't* want something to happen" (p. 6).

As therapists, we want to avoid the word try. If we say, "Try to catch each time you race to a conclusion," we implicitly communicate our uncertainty about whether or not our patient will carry through what we suggest. If we say instead, "Each time you catch yourself racing to a conclusion, notice what fills the moment when you interrupt that push," we communicate a solid belief that our patient will complete the action. The difference in wording is important. How we picture our patient influences how he experiences himself. Our choices in wording convey the pictures we hold of him.

Let us turn to Sylvia's session to clarify my point.

Sylvia was skeptical of my perspective that *her* anxiety about her 16 year old son, Evan, might be amplifying *his* anxiety about himself. If Evan felt humiliated by failure; if he erupted angrily; or if he withdrew into his room in upset, Sylvia became physically dysregulated. "It was *horrifying* to watch him," she said one session, her face grimacing with aversion. "It made me feel *sick, literally sick*, to my stomach; I couldn't stand it. I don't think anyone who isn't there with him in the room when he's like this could understand how *devastating* it is. He is *so* impaired, so *crippled*." There was horror and despair in Sylvia's voice; the emphases in the quote were hers. All she could see was Evan as broken. I feared she was crippling Evan by not being able to loosen the grip of believing he was crippled. Her subjective experience did not fit the data of Evan's growing ability to rebound and restore.

I empathized with Sylvia about how painful it was for her to feel Evan's distress in her gut and feel helpless at the same time. I did not engage in exploring the whys of Sylvia's upset; we had done this many times before and had addressed multiple answers. Nothing had changed. This time I approached doing rather than thinking. I reminded Sylvia that she was not helpless. She could be active. There were things she could do to feel more on top of her own physiology when Evan's behavior stirred her up. There were ways she could question her conclusions with intention and determination. I explained how physical agitation transmitted itself between emotionally connected people. I reminded her that Evan was perceptive and could read her true view of him. Sylvia was receptive, but doubtful. She remained unconvinced that she could or should change her reaction. In the end, Sylvia paddled down the middle of her wish-to-be-collaborative and her lack-of-conviction by saying to me, "I'll try..."

I responded unflappably, "Rather than try, perhaps we could talk about one or two things you might actually *do?*"

In social settings, speaking the truth about the absence of full intent in another person is not considered polite. If someone says offhandedly, "We should try to do this again sometime," as he waves goodbye, we allow the vagueness to pass without comment in order to preserve a gloss of good feeling. But our patient is not seeking a social encounter with us, nor paying us to gloss over truth. Psychotherapy provides more. If we believe that a difficult query might guide a patient out of gridlock, we speak directly even if being direct in this way creates tension. It certainly did for me and it did for Sylvia. However, the startle created by that directness stimulated movement.

The kindness Sylvia found in my face and tone allowed her to take in my implications even though she had tensed. We discussed concrete actions. She could deepen and slow her breathing to lower her heart rate and calm her nausea. She could mentally review the trajectory of Evan's behavior over time to challenge her notion of his being crippled. She could notice what Evan did *after* he emerged from his room in order to consider the notion of recovery and not stay stuck in her lens of collapse. Sylvia's next encounter with Evan shifted in small ways. She reported that she worked hard not to grimace as he yelled; she didn't pursue him upstairs or become solicitous around his upset. I wished she could have shifted more. I wished Sylvia could see Evan as growing rather than as forever damaged. But I reminded myself that this is what growth looks like: tiny, incremental shifts accruing over time.

Yet

"Yet" expands possibility. It extends perspective.

When we suffer discouragement, perspective narrows. We momentarily drop into a younger brain-state, one in which future is only dimly sensed because the concept of time is not grasped (Droit-Volet & Coull, 2015; Piaget, 1946/1971). In such micro-moments of younger mental processing, what is now is all there is. We feel urgency (Peebles, 1983), or paralysis. The more discouraged we become, the more we find ourselves using words and phrases like never, can't, still don't know how to, won't ever.

Shrunken perspective chokes problem-solving. Appending the word *yet* to the end of "can't" statements pries open the chokehold on our ability to think beyond the moment.

A patient insists, "I *don't know how* to talk to him differently!"

We wait a beat, and add, "...yet."

With a different patient, we might suddenly become tongue-tied and think, "I don't know how to help him grasp my point. I have no words; I have no thoughts." If we are lucky, we notice our panic, notice the finality closing down our mind, and realize we need to take a slow breath. "....yet," we mentally add.

Yet breathes space and possibility back into conversation. "Over time," "let's see," and "when you're more ready," are similar catalysts.

Affirmatives Are More Effective Than Negatives

Negations state an idea, and then revoke it. They are grammatically complex, requiring effort to understand. In contrast, affirmatives are simpler. They state a message and let it stand. They focus the listener in a single direction.

When a preschool teacher says to her students, "Walk quietly; keep your hand in your partner's hand," she is speaking in affirmatives.

If she says, "Don't run! Don't touch anything!" she is speaking in negatives. Negations confuse her students by pulling their minds in opposite directions. They hear "run" and "touch," but are asked to think "don't." This requires logic to *un*do directives that have already stirred adrenalin. Accomplishing such a mental feat is difficult for children; it is difficult for adults as well. As Kahneman (2011) explains, "Several psychological studies have shown that people who are simultaneously challenged by a demanding cognitive task and by a temptation are more likely to yield to the temptation" (p. 41).

Creative marketing agents understand the power of affirmatives. Consider the ad slogan, "Drink Responsibly." The alcohol industry recognizes that: (1) the mind swiftly engages with "Drink," because it is affirmative, sensory, easily pictured, mono-syllabic, and a concrete action; (2) The mind is slow to connect with "Responsibly" because it is abstract, not sensory, and is not defined concretely; and (3) Elaborating the ad with colorful imagery of people drinking sparks adrenalin and deepens the sensory sensations of "Drink" by activating the brain's gustatory centers and mirror neuron system. "Responsibly" fades for lack of sensation and imagery. It is an idea only, one which satisfies societal demands and does not interfere with the vicarious experience of increasing consumption (see Smith et al., 2014).

Let us turn to Ellen to look at affirmatives clinically.

"Don't *talk* like that!" Ellen shouted at herself fiercely, her finger puncturing the air for added emphasis. "Stop getting so angry!"

Ellen was stumbling upon unwanted realizations of how her deceased grandmother lived on inside her. Grandmother had ruled Ellen's childhood home with fury. She was disagreeable, suspicious, and belittling. Everyone was intimidated and Ellen grew to hate her. Imagine Ellen's shame when she found herself yelling at people in the same domineering way.

"There I go *again*! STOP it!" she snapped as she feigned swatting herself on the side of the head.

"How would you like to talk instead?" I asked.

"I want to stop being so angry! Stop yelling and screaming all the time!"

"How would you *like* to sound?"

Ellen startled. She said there was a "blank space" in her mind; she had no thoughts. "Ahh," I said. "Blank is good. That means we're somewhere new, somewhere you haven't been before. Let the pictures and words float up, of how you would *like* to be."

It is easier to change behavior when we picture affirmatively and concretely what we are moving toward. When we describe our goals in terms of what we *don't* want to do, we tangle our brain in negatives and change becomes sluggish. Worse, if we picture the negatives in vivid, sensory, emotional detail over and over, we are actually cementing the very behaviors we wish would loosen. Neuroscientists have demonstrated that imagination can create memories at a neural/sensory level (Reddan et al., 2018).

Connotations Matter: Fragile or Vulnerable?

Claire was struggling with me. I was leaning into her strength and the strength of our relationship to press into a tender spot. I was asking Claire to consider what *her* contribution might have been to feeling "f—ed over" [her words] in a recent interchange.

Claire felt her doctor had been flaunting power. This left her steaming. She felt discarded and treated as value-less. I listened. Then I shared my puzzlement over Claire's seeming refusal to take action on her own behalf. I pointed out that when I floated possible ways to respond to her physician's treatment, Claire rejected my thoughts without discussion.

Confused, I asked aloud, "Why might that be?...Is it possible...that however upsetting it is for you to feel put down, that somehow the upset is less threatening than speaking up?"

Claire bristled. "I feel fragile in those situations...I've been so up and down."

I was quiet for a moment, then spoke. "I'm not sure you're *fragile*.... Vulnerable maybe? But are you really fragile?"

Claire was quiet... I stayed quiet with her.

"...I guess you could say vulnerable..." she conceded after a beat.

"If so, let's listen to what *vulnerable* feels like. But vulnerable is different from fragile." I was careful to slow down each word of the next sentence so that its import might soak in. "I don't believe you are fragile any more...A fragile person could not have spoken up in the planning committee and disagreed with a budget that others were supporting. A fragile person would not have organized a walk through France or have been able to say no to people pressuring her to chair a committee. I understand how you could feel vulnerable when the physician seemed to refuse to speak with you directly. But vulnerable is different from fragile."

Language bestows meaning. Claire grew up physically small in a household where tempers flared unpredictably: objects were thrown; people shouted; adults stomped out of rooms. Claire felt in danger and froze or hid below the radar whenever tension appeared. She felt fragile. She felt too tiny to defend herself physically or verbally if someone's ire turned on her. Through her work in psychotherapy, however, Claire had built emotional strength. Her physical sense of herself now needed to catch up with her emotional sturdiness. Doing so would facilitate turning her "Monday maps" into "Friday maps" (see pp. 1–2, this book).

To think of herself as vulnerable instead of fragile would allow Claire to overturn a few of her pre-existing assumptions. First, one can reveal one's injury (be vulnerable) while remaining emotionally sturdy (not-fragile). Second, having power is not the same as being dominating and belittling. Having power can coexist with being empathic and respectful. When Claire reconsidered the experience with her doctor bolstered by these new ideas, she was able to act rather than freeze and fume. She contemplated the idea that maybe he had been under genuine time limitations rather than flaunting domination. She summoned courage to phone the receptionist and voice her needs, without shrinking from a fear of sounding domineering. She understood that her physician's reply would give her more substantive information about his intent and his nature.

Exchanging adjectives changes connotations. This is a powerful intervention.

Harsh Words

An insidious drag on growth is a patient's thoughtless self-attacks. Harsh words corrode, and their corrosion occurs at a physical level. Let me explain.

We become what we speak. In neuro-imaging studies, metaphors activate neural networks in the brain corresponding to the sensation or movement captured by the metaphor: e.g., "he is sweet" activates gustatory centers; "she grasped the idea" activates the motor cortex (Thibodeau et al., 2017, p. 854). When a person calls himself "stupid... sick...hated," he sets off the muscular, hormonal, intestinal, and chemical expressions of those concepts. His muscles adopt the posture and facial expression of a hated person. His gut churns in the way it would if people called him sick. If what we are telling ourselves is subverting who we are working to become, therapy loses traction.

Addressing self-attacks is a priority.

The Whys of Self-attacks

There are multiple ways to understand self-attacks. Each understanding holds a truth. In the psychotherapy process, we work with the one(s) closest to our patient's narrative and his style of learning.

- Harsh self-talk is a habit. Habits are conditioned reflexes. Changing habits requires consistently interrupting the reflex, so that we become consciously aware of doing it rather than its operating outside our awareness. We strive for consciousness because consciousness gives us the power to choose what we do. Choosing wisely takes effort, intention, and practice.

- Harsh words manifest beliefs about oneself. Changing beliefs focuses on highlighting inconsistencies and contradictions in those beliefs. When we can hold contradictions in mind simultaneously, we enlarge our perspective. This allows and compels us to think through and reformulate what we believe.

- Harsh words are holograms of the past. They echo once-lived moments. We cannot change memories, but we can stop reliving them and we can place them into context. To do so, we start by interrupting automatic fragments of memory that replay, such as harsh words. The process of interruption is like throwing grains of sand into a well-oiled machine (I. Rosen, personal communication, October 12, 1979). Interrupting breaks down automaticity, which opens a path for feeling the harshness at a sensory level. Feeling the harshness opens a path to remembering the story those words have been encoding. When harsh self-talk represents memories, such memories involve attack and instinctual counter-attack. To fully transform such attacks, and not just manage them as a habit, therapy needs to touch a patient's pain, regret, compassion, and grieving and feed those feelings into the original raw, attacking feelings.

- Harsh words may be unconscious imitations of people who formed our earliest attachments. Attachment is a lifeline and lifelines cannot be let go easily. "He had internalized her, bad object as she was for him, because as a child he needed her," said Fairbairn (1952, p. 68). Fairbairn implies that we are compelled to hold tightly to those we need even if those persons have hurt us. The process of sorting among threads of attachment for the ones to keep and the ones to let go is a delicate and sober operation. Carrying through such choices brings deep sadness, loss, resistance, and guilt before being experienced as liberating.

- Harsh words can be primitive ways to self-discipline, preempt feared external attacks, or ritualistically manage shame. Such primitive mechanisms are survival mechanisms. As such, they will not be easily relinquished. In fact, they will not be relinquished at all unless alternative ways to manage the challenges of self-discipline, feared external attacks, or shame are constructed to take their place.

Universals of Working With Self-Attacks

Whichever of the lenses we use for understanding our patient's self-attacks, we will need to help him develop certain capacities: (1)

registering that he has turned on himself and registering the cruelty of doing so; (2) tangibly witnessing what speaking differently looks like; and (3) actively practicing speaking to himself in new ways, not merely thinking and talking about it.

Registering

Because self-attacks are automatic, a patient's first challenge is to notice that they are occurring and register their cruelty. We play a critical role in bringing both to a patient's attention. Our spontaneous responses help. Perhaps you involuntarily wince when a patient excoriates himself. Let that show. Wincing expresses our vicarious pain as we experience a patient's hurting himself. When a patient sees us wince, he is forced to reorganize his understanding of what just took place. Perhaps we respond with, "Ouch," to a patient's demeaning self-talk. "Ouch" shakes our patient's obliviousness. As we learn specifics about what our patient's self-attacks embody, we are able to respond with corresponding specificity. For example, "There's that voice again." Or: "Ah, your father just entered the conversation; what is he trying to say?"

Returning to Ellen (from pages 21–22), we join her as she is learning to register her own harshness. Ellen was blazing with contempt toward her neighbor. She discovered herself stabbing the air with her index finger and became horrified. "Look at me!" she exclaimed. "Look at this finger! Look what I'm doing!" Her mouth pulled into disgust. "Just like that woman [her grandmother]," she spat, as she jabbed her finger into the air *more* fiercely, watching it attack. I looked with her, at the finger.

"What is the finger saying?" I asked.

I said "the" finger rather than "your" finger because I saw Ellen startle as she first caught sight of her finger in the air, as if she were shocked to discover it doing something outside of her intent. When Ellen arrested that finger mid-air for us to look at, she referred to it with a demonstrative adjective, "this," rather than a first person pronoun, "my." I referred to her finger in the same third person, in order to join Ellen's subjective reality, stay close to her discovery, and support her spontaneous differentiation from Grandmother through her use of pronouns.

"What is the finger saying?" I asked.

"You do what I say!" "You listen to me right now!"

This is complex. Ellen now recognizes her harshness, which is an accomplishment, but then she uses it to rail against herself for being harsh. My challenge is to bring a tone of compassion into Ellen's discovery.

"Your grandmother was a strong cookie," I mused. "A pretty tough woman."

Ellen paused, her finger aloft. She lifted her face away from memory and looked at me for the first time in minutes. Her eyes locked with mine. "Whoa-a-a...," she said, mouth in an "o." Ellen wasn't sure how to proceed. My comment had created a startle. I had linked two concepts, which up until now had been irreconcilable: Grandmother and admirable. Ellen could not reject the pairing, because the two concepts also shared an indisputable truth: "tough."

Startle creates pause, which opens opportunity for thought.

"What do you mean, strong?" Ellen asked, half defensively, half confused, and one hundred percent curious.

"Well..." I considered her question carefully. "She had clear opinions, and she was not afraid of stating them and letting them be known."

"Hmph," Ellen snorted. "She certainly was opinionated." She drew out her words sarcastically. Ellen was on familiar attack-ground again.

Not taking the bait, I deliberated aloud, "But what puzzles me, is why she always felt she needed to shout what she thought?" I wanted my statement to hang in the air. I wanted to open space for Ellen to distinguish strength and toughness from assault and coercion.

Witnessing What Speaking Differently Looks Like

Registering harsh words is a significant accomplishment, but then we must construct new ways to speak to ourselves. Alternatives do not magically appear on their own. I like to look for fragments of models tucked away inside a patient. I ask if there is a person with whom he felt safe, or whom he admired, as a child or now—a friend, family member, teacher, or someone on TV. Perhaps there was a character in a movie, book, or play, who reverberated in his mind long after the movie, book, or play ended. I then ask the patient what it was about the person or the experience that stuck with him. Be it Tinkerbell, a camp counselor, an early mentor, or a congressman, such lingering resonances are the beginnings of kinder, ennobling ways of treating oneself.

For example, when Ellen became despondent about feeling helpless to do anything other than attack, she looked to me plaintively. "I don't know what else to do—how *can* I act?" Here was an opening.

"Is there anyone in your life who had clear opinions, and wasn't afraid of speaking them, but who said them without having to 'shout'? Anyone you admired...whom people listened to?"

Ellen thought. Her head tilted. Her eyes fixed far away. Suddenly she lit up and swung back to me, "Marie Deschamps!" she exclaimed.

"I don't know her. Tell me more."

"She worked for the U.N.," Ellen explained. "She investigated sexual abuse. She spoke all over the world."

"What about her caught your attention? What struck you? What was it about her that appealed to you?" I asked.

"I can't explain it; it was something about the way she spoke..." Ellen trailed off in discouragement. She felt herself a failure for not having more. I pulled out my phone. "How do you spell her name," I asked.

"Let's look her up." I pulled up images of Marie Deschamps and handed my phone to Ellen so she could study the pictures and feel into what she was seeing. Slowly, her eyes brightened.

"Dignity! Every time she spoke, she had dignity! And look at her face. It's kind. See the softness? But it's firm too. When she spoke, people listened to her." Ellen's voice started to deflate. "...I'm...I'm not sure what I mean by dignity. That's just the word that comes to me..." She apologized, unsure again.

"Let's look up the definition," I encouraged as I Googled "dignity" on my phone. "Worthy of honor or respect; a sense of pride in oneself; self-respect," I read aloud.

Ellen's face softened. Her eyes glistened with a hint of tears. "Worthy of respect...pride, in oneself. Self-respect. Yes. That's it. *That's* what I want."

Ellen was able to finger what her self-attacks were hammering for—dignity and self-respect—through examining her attraction to Marie Deschamps. As she practiced how to live these ideas out in real ways in subsequent sessions, she made discoveries: being direct has nothing to do with being "mean"; owning one's actions does not mean someone is trying to blame me; having humility is not being humiliated.

Practicing

Growth requires "doing." Like all learning, insights in psychotherapy only take root if we practice them. This is such an important concept that Chapter 4 focuses on it. Here, let us take just a brief peek into Ellen's practicing.

Ellen's sister had assigned Ellen, without asking her, to set-up duties for her daughter's bat-mitzvah. After fretting, Ellen texted her sister that she couldn't be counted on to help in that way because her flight didn't get in on time. This was Ellen practicing being direct without attacking. But she was nervous. "I'm so *pushy!*" she said, with a hint of her old disgust creeping in.

"Hmm, well,...when you just now described what happened, the words that were actually going through my head were 'courageous' and 'clear'. Maybe 'firm' too."

When we are in over our head, we can't easily hear how we sound to others.

Ellen's face changed.

"What just happened?" I asked. "A look moved across your face... how did you feel when I said what I said just then?"

"I don't know... I don't know what I'm feeling." It's common to feel confused when experiencing emotions one hasn't had practice with. Because Ellen couldn't wrap her head around emotions at that moment, I broke my question down into the building blocks of emotion—physical sensations.

"What sensations do you notice in your body right now?" I asked.

A quarter-minute went by. Ellen's gaze lost focus as she turned her attention inward. "Calmer," she replied. "The tightness—here, in my chest—[she circled her finger loosely around the middle of her chest in the crevice just above her lungs]—it loosened and let go.... And, look [she pointed to the corners of her eyes with wonderment]—tears...? What *is* that?" she asked, confused by what she was feeling.

"Maybe you're moved? Or touched?"

I didn't know what Ellen was feeling. But I joined her in exploring. I offered a few trial words. She would tell me if they didn't fit.

"...Maybe touched....But there's something else. The tears...they mean there's 'truth' about what you said."

When Ellen practiced saying no to her sister without shouting, she was uneasy. Her no still felt to her as if she might be attacking, in part because she was irritated with her sister for commandeering rather than asking, and in part because she hadn't yet learned the gradations of no, stop, and I don't want to. Practicing, for Ellen, was not a polished transport into the dignity of Marie Deschamp. Practicing is more like practicing the piano. We develop an ear and an ease one note at a time. When Ellen felt me experience her as courageous, she was moved. She felt held with respect and that I understood a truth: that it takes courage to risk something new.

Call Me By My Name

It is remarkable how seldom others use our names when they speak to us. People may greet us warmly, but how often do they name us as they do? Naming has a powerful effect on experiencing ourselves as whole, meaningful, particular, and in the mind of the other. To be named is to exist.

In Madeleine L'Engle's (1973) novel, *A Wind In The Door*, the Echthroi were dark forces driven to obliterate meaning in the universe, through negating and annihilating the experience of mattering. The Echthroi achieved this by "X'ing" or "un-Naming." This was their chief weapon; it made people not know who they were anymore.

L'Engle's insight is potent. When we are not looked at when we speak, or when another acts as if our voice carries no sound, we feel erased. When such experiences persist, a person feels untethered and frightened.

L'Engle's heroes conquered the Echthroi by "Naming," intentionally designating who people were and recognizing their inner nature. Buber (1923/1970), spoke similarly. Like Engle, he understood that humans substantiate each other by acknowledging each other's essence. When we call a patient by his name as we say hello, goodbye, or speak in session, we substantiate him. It is a small choice, yet one with deeply meaningful impact.

Let us move to Awareness.

References

Bateson, G., Jackson, D., Haley, J., & Weakland, J. (1956). Toward a theory of schizophrenia. *Behavioral Science, 1*(4), 251–264.

Boroditsky, L. (2011). How language shapes thought. *Scientific American, 304*(2), 62–65.

Buber, M. (1970). *I and thou* (W. Kaufman, trans.). New York, NY: Simon and Schuster. (Original work published 1923)

Droit-Volet, S., & Coull, J. (2015). The developmental emergence of the mental time-line: Spatial and numerical distortion of time judgement. *PLoS One, 10*(7), 1–20. 10.1371/journal.pone.0130465

Edelman, G.M., & Tononi, G. (2000). *A universe of consciousness: How matter becomes imagination.* New York, NY: Basic Books.

Ewin, D. (2009). *101 things I wish I'd known when I started using hypnosis.* Camarthen, Wales: Crown House Publishing Ltd.

Fairbairn, W.D. (1952). *Psychoanalytic studies of the personality.* London, UK: Tavistock Publications Limited.

Fausey, C.M., & Boroditsky, L. (2010). Subtle linguistic cues influence perceived blame and financial liability. *Psychonomic Bulletin & Review, 17*(5), 644–650.

Fausey, C.M., Long, B.L., Inamori, A., & Boroditsky, L. (2010). Constructing agency: the role of language. *Frontiers in Psychology, 1*(Article 162), 1–11. 10.3389/fpsyg.2010.00162

Kahneman, D. (2011). *Thinking, fast and slow.* New York, NY: Farrar, Straus and Giroux.

L'Engle, M. (1973). *A wind in the door.* New York, NY: Bantam Doubleday Dell Publishing Group.

Peebles, M.J. (1983). Handling psychiatric urgency: Or, keeping one's diagnostic wits in a crisis. *Bulletin of the Menninger Clinic, 47*(5), 453–471.

Piaget, J. (1971). *The child's conception of time* (A.J. Pomerans, trans.). New York, NY: Ballantine Books. (Original work published 1946)

Reddan, M.C., Wager, T.D., & Schiller, D. (2018). Attenuating neural threat expression with imagination. *Neuron, 100*, 994–1005.

Richardson, D.C., & Matlock, T. (2007). The integration of figurative language and static depictions: An eye movement study of fictive motion. *Cognition, 102*(1), 129–138.

Smith, K.C., Cukier, S., & Jernigan, D.H. (2014, September 3). 'Drink responsibly' messages in alcohol ads promote products, not public health. *News Release, Johns Hopkins Bloomberg School of Public Health.* https://www.jhsph.edu/news/news-releases/2014/drink-responsibly-messages-in-alcohol-ads-promote-products-not-public-health.html

Thibodeau, P.H., Hendricks, R.K., & Boroditsky, L. (2017). How linguistic metaphor scaffolds reasoning. *Trends in Cognitive Sciences, 21*(11), 852–863.

Tippett, K. (Host). (2017, October 5). Daniel Kahneman: Why we contradict ourselves and confound each other [Audio podcast]. In *On being with Krista Tippett.* WNYC Studios. https://onbeing.org/programs/daniel-kahneman-why-we-contradict-ourselves-and-confound-each-other-jan2019/

Westen, D. (2007). *The political brain: The role of emotion in deciding the fate of the nation.* New York, NY: Public Affairs.

3   The Value of Awareness

A psychotherapist has to give birth to the psychotherapist within his patient.

—Thich Nhat Hanh, *Peace Is Every Step*

Inside our patient is the knowledge she and we need to help her untangle herself. Only she cannot access it, at least not alone.

As therapists our job is not to pry and drill. Our job is to connect and listen. We invite our patient to learn more about herself than she knows how to know or has been comfortable knowing. We teach her how to become aware of what is inside her. We insure her emotional safety as she does so. Our training and knowledge will help us see the patterns, the obstacles, and the ways out. But first, our patient must let us in.

Awareness is more elemental and more inclusive a process than Freud's free association. Freud concentrated on his patients' speaking aloud the flow of their uncensored thoughts. His was a creative discovery, an intuition sparked by the prevailing theory of Associationism, which understood thoughts within the mind to be linked in chains of meaningful connections. His intuition was fleshed out by observing Breuer employ Charcot's technique of using hypnotic trance like a truth serum and asking patients to say everything that came to mind in trance. Freud discovered there was information inside the patient, outside of her conscious knowledge, that would make sense of her symptoms if only it could be made conscious.

Freud's techniques of getting at information lying outside conscious awareness were refined over decades. Because of the intellectual context of the era and his own personality style, his emphasis remained on left-hemispheric knowing; i.e., linear processing, uni-directional causality, fixity of states, words, and analysis into parts and lists. But as James Lovelock (2019), 20th-21st century scientist and inventor noted, "The 'A' causes 'B' way of thinking is one-dimensional and linear whereas reality is multi-dimensional and non-linear" (p. 15). Awareness responds to the multi-dimensional and non-linear qualities of reality by including

DOI: 10.4324/9781315449043-3

the flow, circling, multi-directionality, simultaneous processing, gist, gestalts, and sensory bodily-rooted experiencing of right-hemispheric knowing (McGilchrist, 2009). Awareness begins with physical sensations, just as consciousness is sensory first, ideational second.

When psychotherapy leans on thinking and putting into words as the only means of learning and communicating, it loses access to right-hemispheric knowing, and the process of discovery becomes stuck. Left-hemispheric and right-hemispheric ways of knowing need to partner.

The Advantages of Awareness

Awareness is a capacity for openness to sensory-perceptual information from within. Such information is not packaged in words. It is embedded in the body and is continually, dynamically moving. Awareness requires physically and mentally slowing down in order to register and track the flow of physical, emotional, and imagistic streams of data. Such data are not known and organized with language (McGilchrist, 2009), yet they are essential to creative thinking and informed decision-making. They are easily missed when thinking is sped-up and rapid. Awareness enlarges scope and allows many perceptions to coexist simultaneously. A talent for awareness may be innate (see Gardner, 1983, intra- and interpersonal intelligences), however, I make the case for intentionally cultivating awareness in patients. The goal is that it becomes an ongoing way of being with oneself when responding to the world, not merely an occasionally used tool.

Awareness is critical to the success of psychotherapy for several reasons.

A Patient's Awareness Improves the Accuracy of Our Hypotheses

Our therapeutic formulations are incomplete; they are merely hypotheses. Moreover, they are *our* hypotheses. They are based on observations made on the details *we* notice from the outside of the patient, which are limited by the theories in which we've been trained. We need our patient's input. A patient's ability for awareness deepens the reach of information that she is able to contribute to the hypotheses-making endeavor.

The beauty of a patient's un-worded, interior information is that it is immediate and spontaneous. It is authentic. It is not re-crafted, translated, or edited after the fact by the part of her brain intent on re-presentation and relying on pre-existing assumptions. It captures information outside her known narrative. Such information is vital to calibrating the accuracy of our formulations. By developing our patient's capacity for awareness, we empower her functioning as the "diagnostic team leader," which Pruyser (1979, p. 255) put forth as a therapeutic ideal.

Awareness Facilitates Initiating New Behavior

Change forces us into the not-yet-tried, the unknown, and the unfamiliar. The unknown will always feel risky, because we can't know what will happen. Our natural inclination is to protect ourselves by scrambling to predict, as if predicting will keep us safe. Instead, it hamstrings us. Why? Because the brain's system of predicting is based on past experience (Kahneman, 2011; McGilchrist, 2009). It concludes that what is likely to happen is what has happened before, and its predictions are accompanied by a feeling of certitude. Such a system is not geared toward opening space for unknown possibilities. Instead, a person sees and hears only the details that support her old expectations, leading her to conclude that her expectations are proven true, even when they are not. From inside such a mindset, patients are reluctant to initiate new behavior. They argue that it will be useless because the same old outcomes will occur. When they are willing to try something new, they frequently decide too quickly that the old outcomes *are* occurring, even when they haven't let the situation play out long enough to figure out if they are right. Either way, growth is stymied and old templates remain in place.

When we want to open space for noticing what we have not paid attention to before, and for noticing what we are unfamiliar with, then we must shift our brain's thinking from prediction into awareness.

Awareness helps us not panic inside new territory. It steadies us on untried ground. Instead of anxiously spinning out oracular dead-ends, we slow down and observe, and from this place, instead of feeling pressured to react quickly, in order to "get it right" or dodge a feared attack, we track what is happening inside us. Such an approach allows novel perspectives to emerge. We become curious, which quiets fear. Quieting allows us to brave a few additional new steps. This feedback loop stimulates growth.

Some psychotherapy patients believe that they cannot attempt anything new until they have exhausted knowing the whys for what they have been doing. This seldom proves true. A patient usually does not need more answers to initiate new behavior; she needs more courage and trust. Answers to whys are only ideas, and only calm the thinking part of our brain, not the doing part. In contrast, living new experiences provides sensory feedback, which is what the doing part of our brain can trust. We have faith in ideas, but we *trust* actual experience. This is an important difference. Slowing down and observing rather than predicting and expecting facilitates the initiation of doing.

Rule-based techniques, such as cognitive reframes or substituting new cognitions for old ones have utility, but one must be sensitive to their limitations. First, thinking differently, by itself, affects only thinking. It does not transform one's sensory, proprioceptive, interoceptive, phenomenological experience of oneself. It is the *embodiment* of new ways of being that are necessary for sustaining change beyond the ending of a psychotherapy process. To achieve an embodiment of new ideas requires zeroing in on the bodily sensations, images, and relational experiences accompanying the new thoughts and new behaviors, and deepening and expanding one's sensory awareness of them. Second, cognitive reframes are designed for particulars, are processed by the brain as formulas rather than as dynamic experience and require mental focus to reapply each time. In contrast, when one embodies a new experience of oneself, one does not need to "think" through particular cognitions each time. Third, cognitive reframes seldom fit all variations of a theme. They can falter when a patient finds herself in the midst of elements she cannot name or describe. In contrast, embodying a new sense of self allows one to move through unfamiliar variations according to a felt gestalt, even without being able to put into words what she is thinking or why she has made certain choices.

In the end, over-emphasizing how to think risks communicating to patients that we overvalue their categorizing, rule-bound, linear, prediction-making processing system, and discount the importance of learning how to hear, assess, and utilize information from their sensory, non-sequential, curvilinear, and process-aware processing system. Linear thinking organizes and fixes in place; awareness is the fount of discovery and the medium for rooting growth (Gallwey, 1974) McGilchrist 2009. Both are necessary; the latter is critical.

Awareness Is Necessary for Sustaining New Behavior in Order to Construct New Models of the World

In order to construct new models for the world (see Chapter Four), one has to sustain relating with others in new ways long enough to absorb the new information coming out of the changed interactions. This is not always easy to do. Inevitably old feeling-memories—body memories (van der Kolk, 1996, 2014)—puncture one's efforts, sometimes permeating one's experience insidiously before one realizes it, no matter how much work has been done in psychotherapy. Old memories float within one's consciousness like certain viruses float in a latent state within the cytoplasm of one's cells. They are activated and released into awareness when external circumstances—it could be a word, a tone, a look—simulate the memories' origins. Once released, these memories can cause us to misjudge a look, slip into certainty about an old belief, or experience a physical feeling of defeat. We lose a chance to experience the new.

Psychotherapy cannot erase painful memories. What psychotherapy can do is develop a person's ability to become aware of their intrusion, withstand their damaging influence, and accumulate new positive memories that offset their impact and relevance. Pushing back against bad memories with self-talk is not enough. One must neutralize their somatic grip with somatically focused methods. One way to do this is through intensifying awareness of the sensory feel of details in the present that are disproving the memories of the past.

In contrast, if a person responds to the grip of old memories by describing the memories in detail, frantically listing what might be causing her feelings, and rebuking herself for slipping, she unwittingly feeds toxicity. Explaining memories vivifies their imagery, which activates the emotions, neurotransmitters, and physical sensations of the original moments. We want to dull the impact of old memories, not reincarnate them. Further, speeding up and analyzing causality switches on the mental-processing mode of latching onto particulars, predicting, and feeling certainty (McGilchrist, 2009). We cannot support this. We need to *un*couple old connections, insert *un*certainty of outcome, and slow mental processing so that our patient can stay with a moment long enough to see and experience what is new inside it. Awareness promotes such objectives.

I am not arguing against employing interpretive insight or mapping causality. Organizing a patient's story into a narrative of causal events, protective strategies, adaptive strengths, and destabilizing conditions is integral in psychotherapy (Peebles, 2012). I am arguing against mapping's being confused with changing. A map is a scaffold. It is not a process. Growth is a process. Process is navigated with right hemisphere-mediated mentation; i.e., awareness.

The Bonus of Self-Regulation

The astute reader may notice that awareness adds the benefit of promoting psychophysiological self-regulation (Schore, 1994), which is essential for sustaining emotional, physical, and relational health. Awareness' approach of noticing reality, rather than striving to orchestrate it, allows a person to maintain equilibrium in high-intensity moments, recapture perspective, and create mental space for choosing and responding wisely. Such skills benefit not only the psychotherapy process. They benefit a lifetime.

The Bonus of Strengthening One's Reality-Sense

Awareness brings another bonus: strengthening a person's confidence in her reality-sense—her sense that what she is perceiving is what is taking place. Recurrent interpersonal trauma, chronic double-bind communication during formative years, and gaslighting by significant others damage a person's reality-sense, creating persistent doubts about whether or not her perceptions are sure or distorted, clarifying or misleading (Kramer, 1983). Developing awareness strengthens a patient's ability to put a finger on her internal sensations, become familiar with their fluctuations, and track their interface with external events. It deepens her trust in internal sensations as valid data and informative. If we cultivate her proficiency in disciplined inference-making as well (see section below), we provide her with methods for gathering data from her sensations and from the external world, weaving that into hypotheses about what is taking place, and testing her hypotheses for accuracy. Awareness plus disciplined inference-making return vigor to a damaged reality-sense.

The Pursuit of Interpretive Insight: One Last Caution

Interpretative insights are shaped by the assumptions of our theoretical home. When we forget this constraint, we risk organizing a psychotherapy around theory-driven inferences. These theory-drive inferences "...occur all the time. They are appealing because they are mental shortcuts" (Peebles, 2012, p. 116). The problem is that when we use them we see our patient through the lens of an idea, rather than through the lens of who she is, and we misunderstand her.

Theory-derived inferences were originally derived from a patient population with whom the theorist in question worked most closely. Our patient may not match that original population at all, or match it only partially. Sherlock Holmes spoke to this: "It is a capital mistake to theorise [sic] before one has data. Insensibly one begins to twist facts to suit theories, instead of theories to suit facts" (Doyle, 1891/1978, p. 13). When Holmes refers to "twisting facts to suit theories," he is not describing a consciously deceptive act. He is implicating the vulnerability of looking only for what our theory tells us is important, and ignoring, not asking about, not noticing, or explaining away something our patient is doing or saying because it does not have a given place in our theory. This is how clinical mistakes are made (Appelbaum, 1977; Groopman, 2007).

Let me be clear: to become an effective psychotherapist, one *must* learn a theory. One must learn a body of psychological knowledge that is an internally consistent, empirically validated, and clinically supported system of thought about human nature and mental health, and one must learn it well. It is not the theory that is the problem; it is misguided fealty to a theory. Fealty dulls one's powers of observation; we tend not to see what is inconsistent with what we were taught. To avoid this error, remember that theoretical knowledge offers guidelines, not gospel. We must question our theory's limitations. We must become knowledgeable about the tenets of other established, clinically validated theoretical schools outside our own.

It benefits our patients to school ourselves in the art of disciplined inference-making (Peebles, 2012). Disciplined inference-making teaches us how to gather data from our patient without bias. It shows us how to weigh the data we gather. It offers a method for testing the accuracy of hypotheses we form.

In addition, it is prudent to ask certain questions of ourselves when working out interpretive insights. For example:

> How else could I understand this?
> Are there questions that clinicians from other frames of reference might ask?
> What haven't I considered?
> Are there details I am ignoring?
> Am I making assumptions rather than asking my patient?
> Am I not believing or adequately weighting what my patient just told me because it runs counter to my theoretical training?
> Have I tended to formulate the same ideas about multiple patients recently?

Questioning ourselves in such ways helps our thinking remain versatile and stay honest (Groopman, 2007). It helps us develop the theory-of-our-patient that fits *her* facts, rather than twisting her facts to fit our theory.

Developing the Skill of Awareness

Awareness is a capacity natural to most of us. We do not have to create awareness in our patients. We elicit it, and then nurture its development. Exceptions may be persons on the autism spectrum or those with schizophrenic illness, for whom there is evidence for brain-based difficulties with this capacity (McGilchrist, 2009).

The building blocks of awareness are: Slowing, Registering, Noticing, Tracking, and Expressing.

Slowing

It is impossible to reason clearly, much less choose intentionally where to step next, when our mind/brain is sped up. When a person is sped up, she tends not to register all that is taking place. A sped-up mind tends to become over-focused or too expansive, neither of which can solve problems effectively. Over-focused is when perception and conceptualization narrow and begin spinning on a hamster wheel of iterative rumination. Too expansive is when too much is being considered as relevant, to the point of a dizzying, out-of-control sensation that feels disorganized.

Speeding up tends to happen when we are anxious or disrupted. It can also happen when we become excited. In addition, people who are overly reliant on language as their tool of intelligence incline toward thinking harder and faster when confronted with something that confounds them. Thinking harder and faster is a form of speeding up.

How does one slow down one's brain/mind?

Recognizing Being Sped Up

First, we have to recognize that we are sped up. Most of us are not used to noticing sped-up thinking in ourselves. Or if we do, we value it, rather than recognize it as a liability. We may think we are being clever and sharp, without fully understanding how being clever and sharp can cause us to miss essential elements, particularly in relational moments. As Sarah Lewis (2014) says, "When one thinks they understand something, the mind edits reality so efficiently that errors can be hard to perceive" (p. 162). A therapist's feedback is critical to helping identify the threshold between considering a matter thoroughly and beginning to spin in our thoughts too rapidly.

Sped-up thinking moves from point A to point D, without describing B and C. When a patient makes such jumps, it can leave a therapist feeling mildly confused, as if she missed something or couldn't follow the reasoning. However, she may hesitate to stop and ask for an explanation because she does not want to seem as if she is not keeping up, or she may feel it important not to interrupt a patient's flow of thinking. However, interrupting can be indispensable for both patient and process. A patient seldom recognizes when she has skipped over steps of reasoning. A therapist's pausing her and asking her to explain provides in-the-moment experience to the patient that she has not been clear. If the therapist comments kindly, "Your thinking is going faster than I can follow. Do you feel sped up?" the patient will naturally pause to check her internal sensations. Doing so helps her identify cues for what sped up feels like to her, cues which she can begin to use as guideposts.

Sped-up thinking also rapidly closes in on conclusions rather than leaving open space for several possible explanations. Jumps to conclusion can be so subtle that it takes practice to catch them in a patient.

Claire showed me a text from her friend, and explained, "It really bothered me, the way she criticized me like that."

"Criticized you?"
"Yes!"
"Where was she criticizing you?"
"There. When she said, 'Where is your anger?' See?"

"I can feel how much her question really disrupted you, just from how you're talking about it. But I'm wondering if you got disrupted, and *then* sped up, and then jumped to a conclusion…that she was criticizing you. I'm not sure I'm seeing criticism in here? Maybe I'm missing something? Tell me what you are seeing."

When I interrupted Claire's conclusion, and helped her slow down enough to detect what particular words had disrupted her, she put her finger on the word, "anger." Claire was offended by the idea that she might be angry. In the second of being triggered by this idea, Claire couldn't think; she could only react. Caught off guard by her friend's question, Claire became frightened; she felt assaulted. In the absence of knowing where the assault was coming from, Claire reflexively concluded that it must be coming from outside her—from her friend—when the assault was coming from inside her. For Claire being angry was an undesirable quality and she had worked hard to make her angry Self a not-me (Chefetz & Bromberg, 2004). She lashed out at her friend for being "rude." Sped-up thinking had misled Claire's judgments about intent; her friend had been puzzled, not rude.

Sometimes, sped-up thinking presents as a patient simply being quick. A patient's speech may lose pauses, leaving little room in which the therapist can respond. The patient's gaze may become fixed and intense. She may be pressured, meaning difficult to interrupt. The therapist in this situation may feel a rising agitation; if too many minutes are allowed to pass, she can feel a bit dazed as well, as if subtle dissociation is setting in (Peebles, 2008). Subtle dissociation can cloud a therapist's mind for many reasons, but one of them is the experience of "too much" in the room. Whether agitated or dazed, truth is often a therapist's simplest intervention. For example: "I'm having trouble taking all this in just now. Can we pause a little, so I can catch up? What you are saying is really important. And it's a lot. I just want to make sure I can really absorb it."

Learning To Slow Down

Once a person becomes familiar with the sensations of speeding up, she can begin practicing slowing down.

Slowing down is shifting into a different mental state. It is like sitting and watching, rather than racing ahead to outpace, outwit, or nail down specifics. To begin, we pause. Pausing inserts space—between words and between thoughts.

Instinctively, people tend to stop breathing when asked to pause. The pausing I am describing, however, does not freeze time. It lengthens it, slowing it down as if gently pouring thick honey. This kind of pause begins with inhaling slowly and deeply, feeling the air moving up into and through the nostrils, feeling the chest and ribcage expanding with the influx of air, noticing the mind stilling as one's focus shifts to the sensations of breath, and then, equally slowly, exhaling, feeling the muscles, in the face, the shoulders, the arms, release as the air leaves the body. A single long breath is enough to begin the pause.

Next, one notices the silence of one's mind during the long slow feel of the breath. It is important to become familiar with the feel of quiet. One patient likened being sped up to "buzzing bees" in her head. Slowing down "quieted" her bees.

Third, body sensations anchor us. One moves attention away from vigilance to thoughts onto sensations in the body. Doing so calms the subjective feeling of spinning. One patient described having spinning thoughts in her head as "going molecular." She gestured with both hands, splaying outward from her temples. She explained: "It's like an explosion, like going nuclear, only it's like my brain is dispersing into molecules and exploding outward." When this patient slowed down and shifted her focus to bodily sensations rather than on her racing thoughts, she felt like "all the pieces are coming back together. I can feel the outlines of myself again."

Fourth, bringing a patient's attention to her experience of being with *us* in the room as she is slowing down deepens the sensory sensations and the emotional impact of her experience, which in turns thickens networks of synaptic firings. Deepening and thickening experience makes it easier to access going forward. Tuning into us with sensory focus activates her mirror-neuron systems responsible for entrainment of psychophysiological processes. Heart rate, blood pressure, respiration rate, and even brain waves begin to synchronize between her and us (Peebles, 2018; Rossi & Rossi, 2006), further helping her calm her psychophysiological state. To draw a patient's attention to us in the room with her, we direct her focus in a sensory-rich way to experiencing our presence, with her, in the room and in the conversation. For example: "Can you experience *me* hearing you just now?....Can you experience me taking you in?....What are you experiencing as you take-in me taking-in you?.... What are you aware of happening in your body as you notice that?"

Slowing down is not an end point. It is not an intervention complete unto itself; it is the first step of developing awareness. Developing awareness is critical to a larger plan in psychotherapy: the construction of new templates of one's Self and the World (Chapter Four). We must slow down before we can register information that contradicts old templates and helps us redefine them. Slowing down is also a first step—for therapist as well as patient—when psychotherapy feels stuck.

It is remarkable how skilled one can become at this through practicing.

Registering

Slowing our mind/brain is the first order of business; nothing else about awareness can be accomplished without it. The Buddhist monk, Thich Nhat Hanh (1991), explains this truth simply: "When we are capable of stopping, we begin to see and, if we can see, we understand" (p. 39).

Next is registering. To register is to allow a full, conscious seeing, hearing, and feeling of the details and sensations occurring in the outer world and in the inner world of one's body. Registering can only take place when our brain is operating *in*efficiently. Let me explain.

Our brain is primed to make swift, efficient assessments of situations for the sake of survival. It scans efficiently; it organizes efficiently, finding and grouping cues it has learned are important. It is particularly alert to cues reminiscent of times we were wounded. It amplifies the significance, accuracy, and urgency of such cues, assigning them more importance than information about the absence of threat, sometimes to the point of ignoring that latter information. Part of its efficiency is to feel certain about its evaluation, even when justification is insufficient.

This type of efficiency is not designed for seeing "outliers" (Lewis, 2014) when it is the outliers we *need* to see—the data we are *not* used to noticing or are not familiar with—if we want to rework our equations for where we can risk, when we can trust, and what is possible. By equations, I mean the theories that we develop as children when trying to make sense of the way people are acting. For example: when I cry, she is irritated and she notices me; when I take care of myself, she is happy and she doesn't pay attention. Whether we call these equations, theories, conditioned responses, mental schema, self-object paradigms, or templates, the concept is the same. The problem arises—and this is a universal problem—when the equations developed by our child mind are not updated by our adult mind, which is capable now, through neural development, of context, nuance, perspective, and an ability to consider simultaneous truths. For example, when Becky from Chapter Two wants to grow into her explorer self, moving toward life with assuredness and awe, she must see *more* than her brain was able to see at age 8. She needs to register how people respond to her now, not just how her mother responded to her as a child. To do so, she has to allow her brain to be inefficient.

I delineate registration as its own step, because remarkably, it cannot be taken for granted.

For one thing, it takes concentration to notice information that does not conform to one's expectations. It is an accomplishment to train one's mind to go against its thrust toward efficiency and to perceive instead the data outside the field it has been programmed to pay attention to.

Second, perception is not simply a matter of mechanics. Our eyes may be mechanically capable of discriminating visual details. Our ears may be mechanically capable of hearing. Our skin may be mechanically capable of registering touch. But our mind launders the perceived incoming stimuli and yields something different: what we subjectively register. For example, years of emotionally protecting oneself by blunting physical sensations can deaden a person's ability to register those sensations. This may show up as a person not registering pain when an injection is administered. Or more complexly, if a person learns in childhood to protect herself from the mercurial comings and goings of affection from significant others by discounting, ignoring, or draining significance from statements of love, then she'll feel no frisson as an adult when someone tells her he loves her. It is important to grasp this: she may literally experience *no subjective sensations, physical or emotional*. She learned to deaden her receptors because registering sensations led to hurt. In psychotherapy, this person will have to *re-learn* to register the ruffling of longing at the edges of her heart and the crackles of fear that swiftly gather to snuff that longing. She will need guidance to register the warmth on another's face, the softening of his eyes, or the reliability of his behavior. Otherwise, she will see a calm face as an uninterested face, a concerned look as a critical look, a quiet moment as a moment of nothing being there, and she won't even know to look for reliability because, for her, capriciousness was what was always inevitable.

The sensitivity of one's receptors may have been inadequately cultivated in childhood. For example, when a child grows up in a household of depression or self-absorption, others are unlikely to engage her energy and pleasure. They do not eagerly seek her words, her feelings, her thoughts. As an adult, this person's sensations of emotion may be underdeveloped. Her face may seem unmoving. She may not flow with the natural rhythms of give and take in conversation as easily as her innate capacities would suggest she could. When her emotions appear, she may experience them as "loud" or dangerous, certainly as uneasy. In psychotherapy, this person will need to learn to register sensations that were never asked about. She will need to re-calibrate her subjective impressions of the sound and impact of her expressions. She will need to learn to welcome and dwell on sensations rather than skirt around them. She will also need to learn to recognize when another *wants* to hear her.

To facilitate our patient's registering *ex*ternal cues, we inquire such things as, "What did he say? What were his words? Are you comfortable showing me the text? What was his tone of voice? What did his face look like?" We pay particular attention to asking, "What happened next?" Often a patient will end a vignette with an emotion-laden statement she or the other said. The patient will let the intensity hang in the air between her and you, as it did for her in the original moment, its emotion filling her with assumptions about outcome. Our asking, "And how did he respond?" or "What did you say next?" unsticks her from unconsciously freezing in the moment and prompts her to continue scanning. More is there than she is accustomed to registering. When working with registering external information, we might also ask, "Is that a feeling inside you, or is that what he said? What are the data?" Such questions guide a patient toward learning to discriminate between what is coming from inside her and what is coming from outside her. If she responds, "It was just a feeling I was getting," we can inquire, "What was it about the words he used, his face, the way his voice sounded that gave you that feeling?"

To facilitate our patient's registering *in*ternal cues, we ask, "What are you feeling?" If she responds with describing emotions, like "anxious," we follow-up with, "Where are you feeling that in your body?" Some patients respond to "What are you feeling," with describing what they are thinking; e.g., "I just don't think she organizes her life very well; it's not what I would do." We can follow-up with, "That's what you're thinking, which is important, but I'm also asking, what are you *feeling*." If a patient looks puzzled, and asks, "What do you mean?" you can say, "What sensations are you noticing in your body...in your muscles, your stomach, your throat, around your eyes...do you notice sensations of warmth or coolness...where?" We may ask, "What are the pictures in your head?" One patient began to report phrases of song melodies entering her mind, unbidden. The words of the song always told her and me what she was feeling. We are seeking to capture information from the kinesthetic, musical, and intrapersonal realms that Gardner (1983) describes as equivalent intelligences to that of words. This is information that goes missing if we only legitimize thoughts and ideas as knowledge.

Noticing

The next step is noticing. Noticing is being aware of the flow of reality. Noticing understands that, when we sit and watch, something arrives next. It is not a tense poising, braced for enduring. It is more a feeling of timelessness, appreciating that demarcating time into segments is a man-made device and not the reality of physics (Rovelli, 2018).

Noticing does not become snagged on a particular moment or race ahead to an imagined moment.

Snagged

Snagging is being swallowed into a particular detail as if it is the end of the story or grabbing tight to one as if proving a point. Snagging on a detail amplifies it to the point of losing perspective. My experience has been that when a patient snags and vigorously tries to persuade me that what she is focusing on is the only relevant matter, she is reliving some aspect of an old paradigm.

Rachel was taking stock of her efforts to get her paperwork in on time. Her eyes filled with tears as she "confessed" that once more she had been given a warning at work for being late.

I pointed out, "This season you alerted your supervisor a week ahead of the due date about your delay, rather than trying to hide from it."

Rachel was on the verge of crying, "But I still got written up."

"I understand. And you alerted her and had a conversation with her about when you were likely to turn in the documents. It was the division boss who didn't accept what you and your supervisor had worked out."

Rachel was still. Slowly she took in a larger view of the situation. Her old, distorted certainty that she was a mess-up had pulled her in like a magnet. My job was to repeatedly return her to noticing everything that had happened, not just the one thing she was snagging on. Doing so allowed Rachel to experience her incremental growth.

Noticing without snagging helps patients loosen the grip of affectively charged, fear-based memories that are suddenly and unexpectedly activated by details in the present. Such memories exert a profound grip on the body. Fear infused events set off survival responses. Survival responses are difficult to decondition because their qualities of fight, flight, or freeze engage multiple systems throughout the body and are programmed to be immediate and automatic (Cannon, 1929; Porges & Dana, 2018). Even when a patient gains command of the *thought* that her fear is based on events that were in the past, every pore of her *body* will still scream to her that doing anything other than fight, freeze, or flee is dangerous. Interpretive insight is not enough. Gaining agency over one's body is necessary as well. Awareness is one of several approaches that helps with this. The ability to notice the streaming of reality, without snagging on one sensation or interchange, is a sensory capacity. It is the ability to feel and let go, to feel and let go.

Frida had been in psychotherapy for two years. She preferred methodical, pointed thinking that built a case for conclusions. It wasn't simply a matter of style. Frida held fast to this form of thinking because it protected her, like armor. Growing up, her family attacked her observations with anger and belittlement whenever the observations did not suit their preferred experience of themselves. Frida learned to speak with flat precision, lining up points of logic like sentries on a rampart. For her, noticing without preparing for attack did not feel safe, because it had not been safe.

In one session, Frida talked about an upcoming family visit. There was no way she would be able to avoid encountering a brother who had emotionally abused her in childhood. She was afraid, but suddenly, she caught unwanted flickers of hope that her brother might have changed. No sooner had she opened up to her hope, than a powerful grip of fear seized her. This fear was physical and deep. "No," she pushed her words out between clenched teeth. "I cannot go there. It is too close to the visit. I won't be safe if I do, if I let myself feel hope. Maybe when I get back. But not now. Not with my trip being just three weeks away. I have to keep my wall up." I paused, considering what Frida was saying, and how much she had grown. It was true that she was putting her foot down and rejecting my invitation to notice without being sucked into her fear as if it were the only truth. But notice how Frida was speaking her decision with clarity and emotion. She was noticing all that was taking place inside her. She was making a considered, and open-ended, choice, not a unilateral, irreversible push-back. Frida was snagged, yes. She could not move further, but she *could* slow down, register, and notice—to a point. She was able to witness and speak rather than fight or freeze. "I understand," I answered. "It is quite an accomplishment for you to experience and hold all that you are feeling right now. What you are speaking is very clear."

Racing Ahead

We also want to notice details without letting our mind race to imagined pictures of how those details will play out.

Noticing without racing ahead means staying with what is happening now, without developing narratives about what might happen later. We cannot know what is going to happen. There are too many moving parts in interpersonal interactions. We are not in control of all those parts. Prediction is impossible. When we try to predict ahead, we are actually looking behind. Meaning: our predictions are conjured out of what has happened to us previously. As a result, predictions actually cause missteps. We respond to what we think the person is going to say instead of waiting to see what he does say. It is a little like moving to return a tennis shot before the opponent has made contact with the ball.

The other person's response will be his response. What we can control is our response. We keep noticing everything we feel and what others are doing and saying, instead of becoming swept up in imagined movies in our head. Doing so grounds us, so that we are able to respond with balance and focus.

Ben had worked in psychotherapy for several years to be able to engage with mature intimacy with friends, family, and romantic partners. He now felt his competence. He had committed to a woman in marriage. However, within 24 hours of the wedding, Ben was panicking. On his wedding day, he had felt more love streaming in from family and friends than he had felt across the entire span of years growing up. It was so unexpected that he did not know how to hold it all. It was so wonderful that he was certain he would lose it. He became distraught. He couldn't sleep. He couldn't go to work. He described to me with jagged breaths his certainty that he was falling apart. He desperately wanted me to appreciate the alarming "reality" that within two years he would be so helpless and emotionally crippled that his wife's family would encourage her to leave him.

Within ten minutes of being with me in the office, Ben calmed. The familiar experience of my understanding him centered him. He slowed down. Inside a slowed mind, Ben began to see a wider vista. He could grasp how his certainty about the future was imagined, despite how deeply real it felt. Ben's body relaxed as he gained perspective.

But then, abruptly, his eyes grew wide, his face contorted, and he began sobbing.

"What's that emotion?" I asked.
"I'm afraid!!" he sobbed.
"Afraid?"

Ben's body shook as he slid into the vortex of his imagination: his wife would leave him within two years.

"Ben. You're racing ahead. Into a future that isn't here, that isn't happening. Can you feel that?"

Ben's body relaxed as he made eye contact with me and brought himself back to the present. "I can do this," he said, calmer and more focused.

"Yes. You can."

"I can do this," Ben repeated, but this time more shakily, with his face contorting.

"What just happened? What is that emotion?" I asked slowly.

"I got scared again. I'm picturing waking up at 3AM, so afraid." He was close to crying.

I spoke slowly. "Feel yourself *now*, inside this room with me. 'I am doing this now' is right. You *are* doing it. Notice your shoulders against the back of the chair, your feet on the floor, your arms resting on the arms of the chair. Feel the comfort of your breath as you inhale air into your lungs and the warmth in your body as you exhale. This is what doing it feels like. Stay with what is happening. Just notice. Each time you bring yourself back to now, you are more able to feel you and notice what is there inside you—your ability, your competence."

Ben connected with me, and with himself, and as we and he repeated this process, he found his way back to himself. From that place of his more wholly experienced mind-body, we could begin untangling together what it was about getting married that had so alarmed him.

Tracking

When we are able to notice without snagging or racing ahead, we can begin to track. Tracking is witnessing the nuances and shifts in our feelings and thoughts across time and situations. Not with vigilant attention. Not with conclusion or blame. But with curiosity and interest.

Being able to track expands perspective further. We begin to recognize patterns. We see context. We grasp how we have protected ourselves. We experience complexity in a hands-on way, which helps us move away from either-or thinking not because we're following a guideline, but because we tangibly feel the complexity of real moments. We notice our impact on people. We see the imprudence of reacting rashly. We perceive our growth.

Expressing

Learning to express what one is registering, noticing, and tracking can be awkward at first. A person's mind might go blank as she struggles for words. If speaking truth was punished growing up, speaking aloud as an adult will feel potent, both in positive and negative ways. It risks triggering subtle flashbacks of danger. The tools of recognizing being sped up, slowing down, and noticing everything that is there without snagging or racing ahead, work together. They form a powerful method for keeping feelings on board as vital information without letting them wash away perspective. They make it possible to think clearly while saying difficult things. Expressing substantiates one's Self.

One can choose when to speak. One can select what to speak. One can decide to whom to speak. For example, initiating important conversations late at night when tired, hungry, and pressed for time is seldom productive. It is wiser at such times to postpone those talks until both parties are rested. There will be time. The acronym, "HALT," promoted by Alcoholics Anonymous, is useful here. I have modified it slightly. "H" stands for hunger and hydration. "A" stands for alcohol or intense affect. "L" stands for lonely. "T" stands for tired. As the number of HALT variables increase, the less governance our brain has over our judgment. When even one of these is present, it is best to pause before speaking.

When practicing expressing, less is more. "Less" means fewer words, one thought at a time, and direct, rather than implicit, statements. When another person does not understand what we're explaining, it will not feel good. It may even create friction. But those uncomfortable moments provide opportunities to develop one's articulation of oneself. Not being understood forces one to find new words and clearer concepts, which in turn forges a more clearly defined Self.

When we feel competent that we can slow down, notice, track, and express, we lose the urgency to control situations and others as a way of protecting ourselves from surprises. Instead, we know we can handle what is unanticipated; we know we are able to slow down, find our sensations, find our thoughts, notice what is going on, and find the words we want to speak.

Awareness is necessary for illuminating the shadows and shapes of our interior world, our world-within. Often psychotherapy feels stuck because our patient is operating from inside a world that is different from ours. We will explore the process of transforming the world-within in Chapter Four.

References

Appelbaum, S.A. (1977). *The anatomy of change*. New York, NY: Plenum Press.

Cannon, W.B. (1929). *Bodily changes in pain, hunger, fear, and rage* (2nd ed.). New York, NY: Appleton.

Chefetz, R.A., & Bromberg, P.M. (2004). Talking with "me" and "not-me": A dialogue. *Contemporary Psychoanalysis*, 40(3), 409–464.

Doyle, A.C. (1978), *The original illustrated Sherlock Holmes*. Secaucus, NJ: Castle Books. (Original work published 1891)

Gallwey, W.T. (1974). *The inner game of tennis*. New York, NY: Random House.

Gardner, H. (1983). *Frames of mind: The theory of multiple intelligences.* New York, NY: Basic Books.

Groopman, J. (2007). *How doctors think.* New York, NY: Houghton Mifflin Company.

Hanh, T.N. (1991). *Peace is every step: The path of mindfulness in everyday life.* New York, NY: Bantam.

Kahneman, D. (2011). *Thinking, fast and slow.* New York, NY: Farrar, Straus and Giroux.

Kramer, S. (1983). Object-coercive doubting: A pathological defense response to maternal incest. *Journal of the American Psychoanalytic Association, 31S* (Supplement), 325–351.

Lewis, S. (2014). *The rise: Creativity, the gift of failure, and the search for mastery.* New York, NY: Simon & Schuster.

Lovelock, J. (2019). *Novacene: The coming age of hyperintelligence.* Cambridge, MA: The MIT Press.

McGilchrist, I. (2009). *The master and his emissary.* New Haven, CT: Yale University Press.

Peebles, M.J. (2008). Trauma related disorders and dissociation. In M. Nash & A. Barnier (Eds.), *The Oxford handbook of hypnosis: Theory, research and practice* (pp. 647–679). Oxford, England: Oxford University Press.

Peebles, M.J. (2012). *Beginnings: The art and science of planning psychotherapy* (2nd ed.). New York, NY: Routledge Press.

Peebles, M.J. (2018). Harm in hypnosis: Three understandings from psychoanalysis that can help. *American Journal of Clinical Hypnosis, 60*(3), 239–261.

Porges, S.W., & Dana, D.A. (2018). *Clinical applications of the polyvagal theory: The emergence of polyvagal-informed therapies* (Norton Series on Interpersonal Neurobiology). New York, NY: W.W. Norton & Company.

Pruyser, P. (1979). The diagnostic process: Touchstone of medicine's values. In W.R. Rogers & D. Barnard (Eds.), *Nourishing the humanistic in medicine* (pp. 245–261). Pittsburgh, PA: University of Pittsburgh Press.

Rossi E., & Rossi, K. (2006). The neuroscience of observing consciousness and mirror neurons in therapeutic hypnosis. *American Journal of Clinical Hypnosis, 48*(4), 263–278.

Rovelli, C. (2018). *The order of time.* New York, NY: Riverhead Books.

Schore, A.N. (1994). *Affect regulation and the origin of the self: Neurobiology of emotional development.* Hillsdale, NJ: Lawrence Erlbaum Associates, Publishers.

van der Kolk, B. (1996). The body keeps the score: Approaches to the psychobiology of posttraumatic stress disorder. In B. van der Kolk, A. McFarlane, & L. Weisaeth (Eds.), *Traumatic stress: The effects of overwhelming experience on mind, body, and society* (pp. 214–241). New York, NY: Guilford Press.

4 Transforming the World Within

This isn't just a new idea. This is a whole new world.

—A patient

In the movie *The Truman Show* (Rudin et al., 1998) the eponymous hero, Truman, has been raised from birth within an elaborate television set, staged to mimic a real world. It *is* his real world as far as he understands it, yet it is peopled entirely with actors. It isn't until late adolescence that Truman begins feeling uneasy. Bits of his situation aren't quite lining up. At first, he rationalizes odd moments to himself according to how people in his world explain them to him: these are anomalies. It's best to forget them. But he cannot stop feeling there is something more, something beyond the world he lives in. An unstoppable urge pushes him to explore until, drenched by a studio-created storm, he clambers up a flight of stairs hidden against what appears to be the underside of an artificial dome. Truman opens a door and breaches the membrane of his studio-created universe. The moment is unceremonious and anticlimactic. Dazed, he walks into a messier, less predictable, larger world.

Truman's story captures the efforts a patient makes in psychotherapy to get outside the world he inhabits—the world-within, inside his head, his personal "movie set" of past experiences—to a larger world unfolding externally in the now. Our "world-within" confines us just like Truman's world confined and blinded him. We have difficulty seeing it is running off a script because it is so dynamic and vivid that it feels real. It is populated with real persons we have met, encountered, and taken in. It holds experiences of genuinely saturated emotion that remain hot spots of intensity. Behaviors we comforted ourselves with long ago still draw us in and bring relief. Our world-within feels like it is everything that is happening right now. In truth, it is merely a holographic, sensory recreation of the past.

There is a larger world of encounters taking place outside the mental bubble of our inner universe. Ideally, this larger outer world of the now feeds new information into our inner world and continuously reshapes its assumptions, expectations, emotional tone, and decisions. However,

DOI: 10.4324/9781315449043-4

unfortunately like a news clipping service, our inner world curates and spins what is noticed; outer information is often not let in. Our inner world runs new people from the outer world through the array of prototypes already familiar and shoves new interactions into categories of previously lived interactions. In this way, our world-within becomes a closed system that keeps reconfirming itself.

When this happens, we, like Truman, are trapped within a point of view. We don't grasp that our personal rubrics for living life and sizing up other people are being calculated from a small set of bygone experiences. If we are lucky, an interaction that contradicts the rules of our inner universe may unsettle us. Whether we investigate that contradiction, or rationalize it away, depends on how comfortable we are with thinking independently and taking risks. And often, it depends as well on whether or not we have been in psychotherapy.

The goal of psychotherapy, all theory turf-battles aside, is to rattle our patient's certitude about his conclusions. When a patient's world-within has become a closed system—which occurs more frequently than we as therapists recognize—our conversations in therapy risk making little lasting difference in our patient's life. Logic alone cannot transform feelings, beliefs, or actions. Sensory experience is necessary. Moreover, that sensory experience has to get past the patient's self-selecting curator. It has to be actually experienced, not overlooked, rejected, or reinterpreted. For both to happen we must focus as therapists on our patient's sensations not just on his ideas. We must make sure that his new sensory experiences, particularly the ones that contradict what he expected, get registered and—this is critical—remembered.

Re-opening a Closed System

To lead anyone anywhere we must begin with where they are. In psychotherapy, this means we enter our patient's world-within, learn its dimensions, and learn the sense it makes living inside it, even if it hasn't made sense to us when viewing it from the outside. We learn what he carries in his heart.

Learning Our Patient's World Within

> Everything you do is telling me the story that has needed to be told, the story inside, the story that has never been heard.
>
> —Anonymous

Feeling Into Rather Than Inquiring

To enter our patient's inner world, we must feel into it more than inquire into it. Feeling into it means seeing (picturing in detail) what he is describing, using our imagination to move kinesthetically alongside him through the actions of his story, and letting the tone of his voice create feelings and moods inside us. Engaging our senses in this way stimulates our right-hemispheric processing, which facilitates synchronicity. Energy waves synchronize between objects and creatures (pendulum clocks, washing machines, crickets) in proximity (Pikovsky et al., 2001) and between humans in proximity as well. Shifts in our heart rate, galvanic skin response, blood pressure, pupil dilation, muscle tonus, gut motility, and brain waves sync up with our patient's (Banyai et al., 1985; Geller & Porges, 2014; Hasson et al., 2012; Linton et al., 1977; McCraty et al., 1998; McCraty et al., 1999; Pikovsky et al., 2001; Russek & Schwartz, 1994; Schore, 2009). Our patient feels the alignment of wave frequencies instinctually whether or not he can word it consciously. It feels as if another person is with him inside his world, rather than detached and watching him from the outside. This by itself is a profound intervention (Schore, 1994) and correlates with a positive therapeutic alliance (Peebles, 2012).

When we shift to right-hemispheric sensory engagement with our patient we also access our cross-modal perception (Stern, 1985) and cross-theoretical thinking (Peebles, 2012). With cross-modal perception, we register our patient's physical movements as if the movements themselves are conversing with us. For example, we may ask, "What are your tears saying?" Or: "Your fist is having clenching feelings. What do you notice when you let your hand slowly open?" We understand that the speed and intensity of our own movements communicate back to our patient. For example, when our patient is crying we don't suddenly cross and recross our legs; instead, we move slowly, in wider arcs, if we must move at all. With cross-theoretical thinking, boundaries between intellectual domains become transpicuous, allowing us to apperceive our patient from multiple theoretical vantage points simultaneously and create interventions combining diverse points of view.

We are interested in the person our patient feels he is, the intentions he assumes others have, and how he measures and obtains caring, worth, legitimacy, and value.

Process

Our patients show us such things better than they can describe them. When we pay attention to process instead of content, we see what a patient is showing us.

The sculptor, Jenny Holzer (1989), put it this way:

> By your response to danger it is easy to tell
> How you have lived and what has been done to you.
> You show whether you want to stay alive,
> Whether you think you deserve to,
> And whether you believe it's any good to act.

The psychotherapist Wilhelm Reich (1945) described it thus: "The *form* of [a patient's] expression is *far more important* than the ideational content" (p. 49, emphases in the original). The psychologist Roy Schafer (1958) echoed both, "We cannot grasp [a story's] full import if we consider only its content, its narrative detail" (p. 181).

How a story is told is the heart of process. Posture, spontaneous gesture, tone, volume, cadence, and pauses are unedited expressions and cannot be feigned (at least not continuously) except by someone with sophisticated psychopathy. Reich used the term, "character armor," to describe a person's patterns of behavior, speech and body posture; he believed these were living choreographies of what that person contended with in his life and how he navigated his challenges. Noticing such bodily expressions is intrinsic to the diagnostics of eastern medicine. It is also the backbone of integrative, western psychotherapeutic methods such as Sensorimotor Psychotherapy (Ogden et al., 2006), Gestalt Therapy (Perls et al., 1951; Woldt & Toman, 2005), Psychodrama (Moreno, 1980), and the Feldenkrais method (Feldenkrais, 1985, 2019).

The tone a patient creates in the room conveys the atmosphere of his interior. If we let that tone envelop us without becoming swept under, we feel the qualities of the relationships held inside him (Peebles-Kleiger, 1989; Racker, 1957). For example, does our patient relate to us as an adversary or a rescuer? Does he position us as a judge to whom he pleads his case? Or does he tolerate us as a bystander who has little useful to say? Does he confide in us trustingly or does he deflect our remarks warily as if he sees us poised to ambush him? Does he experience our silence as soothing him or as abandoning him? The role(s) we find ourselves cast in as our patient talks to us tells us about the types of people inhabiting his interior.

In the process, we also experience the person our patient feels himself to be. Does he enter with bravado or does he avert his eyes in shame? Does he invite us to laugh with him at his foibles or is he numb? Does his every statement contain unfavorable comparisons with others or does he refer to himself kindly and with patience? How does he end sessions? Does he comply obediently, understand respectfully, demand resentfully, finesse charmingly, or assume he can have whatever he wants? His mannerisms help us experience who our patient has had to be in life or who he was told he was.

In the process between us, we also glean some of the rules by which his world-within operates. How naturally—or not—does he presume emotional safety and trust with us and in the world? What qualities are the currency of his world, the traits he repeatedly admires? Celebrity and prestige? Access to power and information? Sexual attractiveness? Kindness and humility? Intelligence? Steadfastness? In his world what do people need to do to be taken seriously? Do they ask directly or do they have to cajole and wheedle? Do they threaten? Or must they be self-deprecating in order to be non-threatening? Do they wait obediently or do they seduce? Perhaps it isn't until one collapses into helplessness that they are cared for? In his world, are interactions symmetrical or hierarchical? Are they reciprocal or transactional? We listen to his stories and experience the dynamic between us to glean such answers. An inverse method is to pay attention to what about us surprises him. Surprise is a clue that we just did something that doesn't fit with the rules of his world-within.

Lynn had a way of being unable to settle into a chair. She spoke softly, rapidly skimming over her words. Her eye contact was intermittent; her glances of me were stolen. Lynn had come to therapy because to her life felt monochromatic. Without a partner, she felt lonely and adrift. Her isolation deepened whenever she thought about being nearly 50 and not having children.

Lynn's growing up years, while financially solid, had been emotionally bare. Six children made for a stimulating environment, though the children's needs were often neglected. For example, it was a sibling who noticed that five-year-old Lynn had no underwear and lobbied the housekeeper to purchase some. Lynn remembered puzzling once, alone on her swing-set, about how people came to be noticed. She had concluded that one had to be sad.

Lynn needed noticing. But despite a year and a half of being noticed in psychotherapy, Lynn seemed unchanged. This made me uneasy because if I was not making a difference in her life then I was not helping her in the way she deserved and frankly was paying me for. I went over our interactions in my mind. I was listening to Lynn intently. I tracked carefully and reflected back what I heard. I spoke to her strengths. I asked questions. I connected aspects of her history with her feelings in the present. I offered concrete suggestions. I brought emotional energy into the room. I made a referral for medication. But all of what I provided seemed to roll off Lynn and make little impression, like raindrops beading off wax. One day I asked Lynn, "What is your experience of *me*, listening to you now? What is your feel of what is going on inside me when I said that your advice to your colleague seemed thoughtful and creative?" (I was opening a discussion of process.) Lynn looked at me directly and hesitated. "I just assume you don't really feel that way."

I startled. "How do you mean?"

"People say all kinds of things that aren't what they're thinking. I watched that in my family. You have to be nice to me. But I don't believe that you feel it. You're just trying to do therapy and help me."

I wish I had asked Lynn sooner about the process between us. On the other hand, she might not have been able to be frank with me earlier. Therapy had felt stuck because from inside Lynn's interior nothing I did or said was authentic. It wasn't easy for me to go into her reality because it wasn't how I wanted to be experienced. But I knew I needed to start where she was. The point was not for me to convince her that I was genuine. I needed to stand beside her, look around, and see the contours of her universe, one in which "helpful" conversations were really deceptions that hid neglect. And as it turns out, it was my accepting her experience of me as insincere that made me different from others who filled her interior. To Lynn, *this* felt like being noticed. This is what gave her *sensory sensations* of having someone's concern. Lynn's sensory experience of a different kind of person was evidence that her closed system momentarily opened up. It was a step toward new types of people being able to permeate her world-within.

Themes

Another way to learn our patient's world-within is to listen for the themes.

People's interiors are governed by only a few key themes. These themes play out over and over, with different characters, different dialogue, but the same struggle, the same endings, and the same take-aways. For people to feel hope, the themes of their interior must change or else they keep expecting (and unwittingly recreating) the same sad endings. Epiphanies are those moments of sharp clarity when story arcs crystallize into new trajectories.

To detect a patient's themes, we listen to their stories in a particular way: rather than drilling deeper into the details, we settle back, so that our ears catch the music.

In our first session, Elena identified each adult in her stories by their advanced academic degrees. Intrigued, I mentioned this. Elena felt disconcerted; she hadn't been aware she was doing this. Associations tumbled out. She was ashamed of not having a graduate degree. In her world, he who is quickest is smartest, and he who is smartest gets listened to with respect. Advanced degrees, prestigious schools, and media recognition seal the deal. Those without? They are ignored and discounted as not worth much. Elena strove because she did not feel she measured up. Yet Elena was already quick as mercury, with rapid, often brilliant, insights. The sadness was she felt confused and defensive about not "accomplishing" more.

Elena's experience of herself as not-enough to merit attention emerged as key to our work. She had a younger brother with hyperactivity and early drug abuse whose needs had sapped her parents' energies. Her father was consumed by his responsibilities as CEO of a large corporation. He would greet her warmly when he arrived home from his travels, but that warmth lasted only as long as it took him to walk from the front door to his study. Elena had to spill her ideas quickly during that journey from doorway to den.

Sitting with her in my office, I experienced Elena differently from how she described herself. She was deeply compassionate. She was playfully creative. Her connecting of disparate ideas was sometimes astonishing. It was as if these aspects of her had not been commented upon as she grew up, so she had not assimilated them as being her. Witnessing her qualities aloud and buttressing my observations with specific examples began shifting Elena's relationship with herself. She began valuing her comments. Gradually, because she felt she was saying something worthwhile, she spoke with fewer distractions and qualifiers. In turn, people listened to her more and Elena felt worth listening to. Elena was feeling her competence in a sensory way. She was still vulnerable to the old sensations of inadequacy, but now she had tangible new sensations to gravitate toward and use for steadying.

Emotional Intimacy

Emotional intimacy is another means by which to learn the interior world of a person.

Childhood attachment patterns activate inside adult intimacy. Our original intimates are our earliest caregivers. They create our template for attachment. Their reactions when we approached and needed them, our feelings in response, and the ways we managed our feelings, determine how wary, clinging, withdrawn, or assured we behave as adults with intimates (Bowlby, 1969; Fonagy et al., 2002; Goldberg et al., 1995). Because attachment experiences are physical and sensory, our caregivers' energies of rejection or welcome encrypt in our bodies. We elicit behavior from our romantic partner that matches what we grew up with. We do so through the ways we behave, expect, interpret, and accuse (Horwitz, 1983; Rosenthal & Jacobson, 1968). It takes a grounded partner to resist the dances of old memories with us. It takes an aware person to learn how to not keep inviting the other into these old dances.

A therapist who is able to engage with emotional intimacy in the psychotherapeutic process, in intentional and regulated ways, unlocks unique access to his patient's interior world (Peebles, 2012; Shectman & Harty, 1986). Engaging in this way requires training and disciplined subjectivity (Erikson, 1957/1964; Peebles, 2020).

Ben came to psychotherapy with shaky self-confidence. Taunting and physical assaults by peers during childhood left him frightened that he would be attacked if he went against the crowd. Therapy helped Ben begin risking standing out again. Managers at work began counting on him as a leader.

As discussed in Chapter 3 (pp. 44–45, this book), three years into the work Ben's growth abruptly collapsed. 24 hours after his wedding, panic struck like lightning. He could not sleep. He could not function at work, which escalated his panic. He lay in bed, asking his wife to hold him. He phoned his mother in the middle of the night seeking her consolation. He sought medical consultations for sensations that troubled him and moved about in location and intensity—numbness, pains, perceived loudness of his heartbeat. Despite people's concern and help, Ben was convinced that no one cared about his terror; nobody believed him; and nobody was committed to penetrating his isolation. I made a referral for pharmacotherapy and increased the frequency of his psychotherapy sessions.

Clarity emerged only slowly, across several months. The step across the altar, the cold metal of the ring sliding onto his finger, and the white noise of congratulations had kicked Ben into sensorial memories of being trapped in the home of his childhood. Home was isolation, being forgotten, and not connected with emotionally. It was a place of closed doors, dark corridors, and cold. It was where he had lain on his bedroom floor sobbing. The ring became a handcuff locking him into a nightmare.

The atmosphere and tone of one's childhood home are seldom worded. Instead, they encode in sensory sensations and are remembered in sensations and actions. Ben felt he was "losing his mind" because he was feeling without knowing why and believing truths that were not logical in the now. When one is without words, he can feel as if he has lost hold of his "mind" because we inaccurately equate mind and thought with language (McGilchrist, 2009). Ben's mind was fine. We just needed to decipher the knowledge arising from his senses and translate that into words. It is not that words are better or more accurate than sensory experience; words and sensory experience partner. Words create frameworks of thought that allow for perspective, context, and temporal organization. As Ben began speaking his memory rather than living it, his mind could untangle the sensory confusion between "home" as it existed in his childhood and home in the now of his marriage. Slowly Ben recovered.

"Hand Me Down Blues" (Yapko, 1999)

The mood and feelings inside a patient's interior are not always his own. Before full myelinization of the frontal lobes in early adolescence, a child cannot fully differentiate himself from emotions swirling about him; he is unable to fully critically vet and govern what is let in. Experience becomes absorbed, not named; sometimes what is absorbed are emotions emanating from the adults outside him. Depression, fear, anxiety, and manic stimulation create physical sensations in a child's body, and a child does not know to separate his Self from such sensations. Through such portals, a parent's depression soaks into a child (Yapko, 1999). There are other ways a child's interior is permeated with feelings and moods from outside him. Sophisticated aspects of the mirror neuron system (Iacoboni, 2008) activate modeling of parents' emotional behavior; family dynamics slot children into emotional roles that complete the family ecosystem; there is even epigenetically mediated absorption through secondary DNA transcriptions (Lehrner & Yehuda, 2018; Yehuda, et al., 2018). It is important to be aware of such processes so that (if necessary) we can help a patient distinguish his innate nature from what has infiltrated his interior from others.

Putting Awareness to Work

After we have met our patient where he is, entered his world-within, and learned the sense it has made for him, we need to help him open the membrane of his world to outside information; i.e., convert his closed processing system to an open one. He needs to notice things he is not used to looking for before he can experience himself and others differently. Taking in new information does not happen automatically. It has to be learned and practiced intentionally.

Here is where our patient realizes the benefits of the skills of Awareness (Chapter 3). When we slow down our minds, we are able to look longer and scan more broadly. Doing so enables us to see details and data that our world-within has trained us to consider irrelevant.

Consider our movie hero, Truman. At one point a large stage light hurtles ground-ward from the unseen rafters of the studio set and crashes near Truman as he's about to get into his car. Startled, Truman edges closer to investigate. The strange writing on the canister confuses him: "Sirius (9 canis majoris)." It is the stage light dedicated to mimicking that star when night comes to the set, but Truman doesn't know this. He has no template by which to evaluate this strange occurrence. At least he noticed it: he neither ignored it, nor dismissed it. He allowed himself to slow down, register, and investigate.

However, now Truman needs to reason outside the box of his inner universe, and this is where opportunity gets quashed. When a befuddled Truman returns to his car, he hears a "news flash" (quickly scraped together by the producer) on his car radio, "An aircraft in trouble began shedding parts as it flew over Seahaven just a few moments ago. Luckily no one was hurt." Truman is offered a rationalization by which to dismiss the anomaly. He was able to perceive the unfamiliar occurrence, but he was stopped by the producers of the show from pondering outside the known tenets of his world when explaining it. The producers succeeded in that moment; Truman's processing system remained closed.

To open a closed processing system we need to perceive more, *and* we need to be able to reason flexibly, not rigidly. Awareness with its slowing, noticing, and tracking is essential to accomplishing both.

Becky tensely described how angry her supervisor had become when Becky sought help about a disgruntled client who had brought a sizable portfolio to the firm. The supervisor, according to Becky, was upset that Becky was not adequately managing this client's demands. Becky felt a familiar fear: she was caught between two people, neither of whom she could please. It could be argued that my best therapeutic path was to explore the historical roots of Becky's fear. One could also make a case for my working with the logic of Becky's reasoning. Equally valuable would be if I provided empathic understanding. Each path has merit, and they are not mutually exclusive. I chose to move to the building blocks of perception. Becky and I already knew her fear. I was reluctant to have her feed her mind and body with more doses of that fear through vividly describing its historical details again. I wanted to help her expand her world-within by becoming able to take in new information. "What did your supervisor actually say? What were her words? Can you describe the expression on her face? What was her body doing?" I was not challenging Becky's reality; I trusted her experience. I was encouraging her to look again, this time more slowly, and see what else might be there.

Once we see something we hadn't noticed before, it is important to *feel* that new piece so that the body has an experience of it. This is the noticing from Chapter 3. New details that don't fit our familiar script tend to land in the thinking mind instead of the feeling mind. "Yeah, yeah," or its equivalent is a common response from a patient to a previously unnoticed detail. If we leave it at that, the new piece won't soak into experience, and experience is the essence of the world-within. To create experience, we redirect our patient's attention to the thing just noticed and ask them how it *feels* to be aware of it. We ask them to linger in the feeling so the moment prolongs itself as a sensory experience.

During her lifetime Ellen avoided emotional friendships because, in her interior, friendships were not safe, and women attacked her with barbs that cut like razor blades. One Sunday, a woman came up to her in the church vestibule and blurted, "I'm just so glad you're part of our community now." Ellen was dumbstruck. "I didn't know what to feel," she told me. I suggested she take a second and replay that moment in slow motion in her mind. "Notice the look on the woman's face, the sound of her voice as she speaks those words to you, and the sensations in your own body as you feel her facial expression, her body language, and her words soak in. What are you most aware of as you see and feel that now?" Ellen reported a loosening and calming in her chest; tears unexpectedly came into her eyes. Feeling emotionally touched in this way was a physical sensation that had been blocked out by years of Ellen's bracing when women moved close to her.

Focusing On Experience Not Just Words

Once we are able to notice and ponder people and interactions that challenge the expectations of our personal bubble, we must focus on the sensory feel of these unaccustomed realities and we must rehearse those sensations. To become a living part of our interior, they must feel real to us in a physical way.

Inhabiting a New Self

An infant's first reference points are sensations. Everything that composes mind and Self grows from there. If caregivers fail to respond to a child's sensations and expressions, the infant's nervous system becomes dysregulated and he loses organization of his body and his feelings (see video: UMass Boston, 2009). If the failure to respond continues, the child becomes listless and may even stop growing (Spitz, 1945). Less extreme but equally formative is when a child is scolded into ignoring emotions. Eventually he no longer feels their physical sensations.

Cathy was sensitive and curious as a child but her Calvinistic upbringing eschewed displays of feeling and rewarded logical debate instead. Among the five children, those who could argue theology most deftly with father were praised. Feelings were not simply annoying; they were considered tedious and uninspiring. Cathy, the youngest, was mocked when she cried. Decades later, when I asked Cathy how she felt about something, she would add details to explain her point, not feelings. When I asked what she wished would've happened, she articulated the most prudent path forward, not wishes. In Cathy's inner world, her Self concentrated on intellectual prowess. A quick mind was a safe mind.

"I asked what you were feeling actually, not what you were thinking," I gently pointed out.

Cathy startled and looked confused.

"What is your emotion just now?" I encouraged. When she continued to look unsure, I shifted my question: "What do you notice feeling in your body?"

Cathy had trained herself not to notice emotions because she had been attacked by her family for showing them. To not-notice emotions she had needed to dull consciousness of their physical sensations. Inviting Cathy's sensations into our conversation was our first step in altering her inner experience of herself. If Cathy could reclaim sensations, and through them her emotions, and eventually embrace both as rich rather than shameful, then her natural sensitivity, tenderness, and delight might be returned to her.

Other patients may have access to their sensations but dissociate from them. To become themselves again they must *feel* themselves again.

June, an experienced actor, carried the principal role in a play at a leading theatre. The show rose or fell on her character's emotional verve and presence. Opening night, as June prepared to speak her first lines, she was suddenly seized by an out-of-body experience. "How do I know these lines?" she mentally gasped. "How is it that I'm walking here, not over there? How is it that I know what to speak next?" June's heart pounded. Instinctively she knew that her lifeline was to connect with the concrete sensations in her physical self. She prompted herself to fix her gaze on her co-actors' eyes in order to physically feel the energy of each person's response to her. Tangibly tapping into her co-actors' responses toward her helped June feel her own body again. From there she was able to find her way back into the spirit of the woman she was portraying.

If a patient cannot feel cues from his body, directing him toward noticing his breath is an accessible starting point. Sharp tactile sensations (stretching, standing up, moving about the room, cold water on one's face or hands) or smells (citrus, peppermint, tea tree) are additional ways to jump-start physical awareness.

Some patients can feel their body's sensations but are sensitive to the point of porousness, which brings its own difficulties integrating new experiences. The clarity of their Self dissolves when flooded with emotions. They feel unsure of whose emotions are whose. "Are you angry or am I angry and thinking you're angry?" "Did you just criticize me or is that me attacking myself?" "Is that what *I* want, or am I reading what *you* want?" One patient described it as "losing my mind," meaning she was losing hold of what *she* felt, thought, or wanted. Without confidence knowing whose ideas and feelings are whose, people have no way of crystallizing information about who *they* are. They become spun around in eddies of reactivity and self-doubt.

Elena explained in desperation that she had to keep my ideas out of her head in order to know what her own thoughts were. Her mother's double-bind (Bateson et al., 1956; pp. 16–17, this book) communication style had operated as a sort of "confusional trance induction" for her as a child (Erickson, 1964/1980; Otani, 1989). It had the phenomenological effect of "depositing" ideas in Elena's head, bypassing Elena's ability to critically screen the ideas. Years later the effect on the psychotherapy process was that Elena was constantly pushing my comments away, neutralizing their impact with instant argument. It wasn't because she disliked me; it was her survival tactic inside intimacy. When Elena felt emotionally open she became afraid of becoming mentally porous. She argued to prevent others' ideas from getting inside her head without her consent.

Our first order of business had to be helping Elena firm the contours of her own mind so that she could consider others' ideas without losing hold of her own. Elena was easily riveted by interpersonal cues so I slowed my facial reactivity and head-nodding. I wanted to clear her visual landscape so that she could feel her own thoughts before she began anticipating mine. I explained what I heard Elena to be saying rather than responding with my ideas. I used her words, eliminating synonyms and metaphors that might feel like I was shading my meaning over hers. I repeatedly emphasized her right to authorship: "What I hear you saying is X. Is that correct? Am I understanding you correctly or am I a little bit off?" I worked to eliminate inflections that might sound like subtextual messages. I introduced observations with, "I'm wondering if…" and added at the end, "What do you think?" Working with Elena in this careful way brought her thinking into sharp relief for her and provided her with a sensory experience of holding onto a thought without its dissolving. By doing this we gradually eased off the stuck point of Elena's needing to argue away my comments. She became able to consider ideas I offered even when they were ones she had not thought of first.

Some patients may feel very clear about their feelings and who they are but their perceptions of themselves are distorted. These distortions were sown by significant others at an early age.

Becky became frozen with shame and guilt while telling me she was upset with her mother. She was horrified she felt this way, so much so that she could not make eye contact with me.

"Say more about the shame," I invited.

"I'm unkind. I hate being unfair to her like this. She loved me so much. What I'm saying is mean," Becky replied, staring at the floor. "I literally feel like I'm shrinking."

Becky was not wallowing in self-attack. She felt genuinely pained by perceiving what a bad person she was convinced she had become. Experiencing this turn of events left her unsure about whether or not continuing psychotherapy was a good idea. "I've felt so helped by therapy, but now I'm turning it around to blame my mother. She doesn't deserve this."

Slowly I unspooled the threads of Becky's feeling with her, word by word, picture by picture, until associations and memories floated atop each other like superimposed transparencies. The image that crystallized Becky's knot of shame was this: she remembered watching her younger sister Karen push mother away when mother began playing in Karen's doll house moving figures. "Get away!" Karen, who was barely three, swatted her mother, who burst into tears. Time seemed to stop for Becky. She remembered her father running in.

"She needs to apologize!" sobbed her mother.

"What happened?!" Father asked worriedly.

"She pushed me away. In such a hurtful, mean way. She's so unkind," her mother gulped between sobs.

Becky remembered feeling frozen and "weird." Her mother seemed "out of control." Nothing about that moment had seemed like Karen's fault because Karen was so young. As the memory unrolled in Becky's head, she saw Karen's face: first startled, then a nanosecond of confusion, and finally bursting into tears as if dissolved by shame for being such a bad girl for making mommy cry.

Watching this memory in her head Becky could hear her mother's voice and see Karen's confused dismay. Slowly Becky felt something "drain off" from her. She felt "relief," like a "freeing." "I wasn't bad," she said slowly, her eyes still far away fixed on the memory. "Something happens inside my mother when she feels rejected. It's inside *her*. It's not me." In real time, Becky's physical, emotional, mental, and tactile experience of who she was as a person reorganized. A new perspective, felt physically as a larger, freer bodily sensation, allowed Becky to feel frustrated with her mother yet forgiving of her too. She no longer felt herself as mean.

The path to helping a patient reorganize his sense of Self does not always take cathartic turns. Sometimes the steps are surprisingly pragmatic.

Kinsey grew up an only child, isolated on the outer edges of her rural school district. Her mother was severely depressed and spent most days in bathrobe and slippers, abed or stumbling through the house. Sometimes supper was a bowl of cold cereal. Her father worked in construction and stayed away, typically coming home late after drinking. There was little money. Kinsey did not want friends over for fear they might see the desperation in her household.

When Kinsey would screw her courage to ask for something material, father called her selfish. "What's wrong with you?" he'd snap when Kinsey confessed her dreams of having more. She learned to be silent about wishes. Decades later in therapy Kinsey complained about a constant lethargy and malaise. Through hard work and fortune, she now lived in wealth. But her inner world remained engulfed in isolation and silence. She continued experiencing no one listening to her wishes. By now she had forgotten how to speak them.

I pointed out how Kinsey's listlessness echoed her childhood world living inside her. She acknowledged my logic, but the observation fell flat. It wasn't until I worked closely with the details of Kinsey's daily life that she began to awaken. For example, she was uneasy with her hairdresser. He was insisting on cutting short layers and bangs and he took offense when she timidly suggested letting her hair grow out. Kinsey felt cowed and silenced by his arrogance. We spent weeks discussing Kinsey's discomfort with not being heard by this man. Inside her inner world there was nothing she could do. If she left him, where would she go; his expertise was unmatched. If she stayed, she suffered. We discussed strategies. We role played what speaking directly to him might look like. She researched other stylists. Slowly Kinsey extricated herself from her stylist and found an equally talented person who listened and carried out Kinsey's vision.

Service provider by service provider, from hairdresser to housekeeper to interior designer to building contractor and eventually to friends, Kinsey and I painstakingly developed her ability to respect her thoughts, to speak them even when afraid, and to move away from people who did not listen and toward those who did. In one session, through tears of anxiety, Kinsey risked telling me that I had been asking her questions for 20 minutes about something she did not care about. She had been eager to talk about something else. Now the time was nearly gone. I paused, listened carefully, then thanked Kinsey for letting me know. "How much you've grown that you could risk believing that what you wanted was worth saying to me. I'm so glad you told me. I never would've known otherwise."

One might dismiss this therapeutic process as superficial. Hairdressers? Housekeepers? Interior designers? But for Kinsey, learning the childhood origins of her malaise had not freed her because it was a lifeless idea, not a felt experience. Kinsey needed to live out being different in order to feel different, and her being different in the now reshaped her sensory experience of her Self in her world within. Kinsey no longer felt listless; she felt alive.

Expanding a Picture of Other People

When a person has never had certain interpersonal experiences, it takes intention to perceive them now and to let them permeate sensorially as real.

Tanya's childhood world crackled with angry people. She learned to coil inwards to protect her sensitivities, but she ached for connection. As a child, she spun a magical way to feel held by people who cared: she built a collage of photos of emotional, caring women from magazines. She hid her treasure under her bed and pulled it out when in need.

When Tanya came to psychotherapy, her mind was sharp and wary, but her heart was hurting and vulnerable. She could not receive people easily. She saw micro-movements on people's faces accurately, but her processing would speed up and she would misinterpret attack based on inner assumptions. Every shift of my face amplified threat for her. I was rejecting her. I was angry and sick of her. If I seemed supportive, it only meant I'd been fooled by her. Tanya's photo collage had been a safe haven. Real people are fraught. Pictures don't talk back. Their faces don't move. There are no voice tones to sort out.

Most of Tanya's energy in therapy was being spent bracing against the next threat I might pose. There was little left to focus on herself. I tried everything I knew to do. I discussed what I noticed. I mindfully slowed myself down. I tried to help her slow herself down. I linked her responses to her history. I encouraged her to sort out the data logically. Tanya understood and tried hard, but she kept being swallowed by her inner world's certainty. As McGilchrist (2009) put it, "Our incapacity to see the most apparently obvious features of the world around us, if they do not fit the template we are currently working with, is so entrenched that it is hard to know how we can ever come to experience anything truly new" (p. 163). Our process felt stuck.

I talked with Tanya about our challenge. I suggested we consider her difficulty from a perceptual and processing point of view rather than as something pathological. Seeing me was flooding her with sensory information. She needed to wrestle with less information perceptually so that her mind could relax and learn how to use a relationship to sort through what was taking place. I could not become a flat picture on a collage for her; neither of us wanted that. What if we put a temporary barrier between us that eliminated some interpersonal cues, but not all? What if she could still hear me but did not have to contend with seeing me? I suggested we borrow a tool from psychoanalysis: she would lie on a couch and I would sit behind her. This might help me as well. I might be less drawn into an escalating spiral of mutual interpersonal reactivity if I weren't being watched so closely and if each of my movements didn't count so much. Tanya responded by worrying that not being able to see me might tumble her into the unbearable aloneness she had felt as a child. It was a reasonable worry, but I reminded her that she would have my voice to tether her and that we could pay close attention to walking her through any reactions of that sort. And of course, our use of the couch need not be inflexible.

The couch helped. It served as a bridge between the virtual intimacy with her collage that had felt safe for Tanya and the living intimacy with a person. Interactions between us still unfolded, and Tanya still froze, suspecting I was silently angry with her and wanted myself rid of her. However, her external cues from me were limited to my voice tone, inflections, pacing, and language. She did not have visual information from my eyes, facial muscles, and head tilts. Less information to account for and interpret meant her brain scrambled less frantically and thus was easier for her to slow down. Tanya's slowing meant she could pause to gather data that supported or refuted her reflexive conclusions about me. When watching me from the chair, each new micro-movement on my face had heightened her alarm, which had sped her to concluding. From her refuge on the couch, Tanya learned she could go back and examine my tone and my word choices to see if they fit or contradicted her fears. She learned to pay attention to *how* I interacted, remembered, and responded as valid information about if I had turned her away in my mind or was taking her in. She learned to risk asking me questions as another way to test out her assumptions. She learned to feel the sensory information coming up from inside her body and employ it as another form of data. The more alternative methods she developed of checking out her assumptions, the more her vigilance relaxed. As her vigilance relaxed, Tanya gained access to images and phrases bubbling up organically from her right hemispheric processing. All these abilities strengthened Tanya's sense of Self and opened her to the experience of me as a person different from those who previously populated her interior.

After two years Tanya left the couch and returned to the chair opposite me. She was now better able to stay present with her uneasiness when she perceived something on my face because her body had accumulated physical sensations of my constancy and acceptance of her. She had developed methods of looking for more information inside and outside herself. She had developed the courage to ask questions rather than race to silent conclusions. Tanya's story illustrates my concept of working with the "seeds of an alliance" (Peebles, 2012).

Redrafting the Rules of the Interior

People's beliefs and decisions emerge from an internal, personalized calculus about what is important and therefore how the world should work. Family, culture, community, and religion imbue children with their inner rules at a very young age. These rules determine what constitutes success to a person, what makes one lovable, the advisability of taking risks, the attitude toward mistakes, the responsibilities we have to others, and how much control we have over events. We are convinced that as adults we arrive at political, social, and religious decisions with diligent study and logic. The truth is our beliefs flow at a deep level from our heritage (Kahneman, 2011, Tippett, 2017) and are intrinsically emotional rather than logical (Westen, 2007).

It is human nature to move along as if the snow globe in which we live is the same one everyone else is living in. Psychotherapy can feel stuck when patient and therapist are proceeding according to different sets of internal rules but don't realize they are doing so.

Lynn and I were relating to each other from different assumptions about how the world operates (pp. 52–53, this chapter). Lynn believed that what people say is not what they are thinking. I assumed that what I say *is* what I am thinking; I may not speak everything I am thinking, but what I speak is truthful. Lynn and I were stuck until we discovered how different our interior rules about engagement were.

Similarly, Claire and I were experiencing my interventions very differently and did not know it. When Claire would describe an interaction that distressed her, I assumed she was asking for my help in navigating it. However, Claire was not asking for help. From within *her* interior, her descriptions were shameful confessions about her inferiority. She experienced my "help" as affirmation of her being deficient. I was clueless about this and blithely kept responding with more "help." I can't explain my cluelessness, and it is a good reminder of how blind we can be to the possibility of others' different underlying assumptions, as well as our blindness to the legitimacy of those assumptions. I could point to Claire's nodding assent when I would speak and the widening of her eyes as she confirmed that what I was saying made sense. However I didn't pay enough attention to my discomfiture with how her agreement always came just a half second too fast, with a tad too much nodding. I finally let myself take my unease seriously and I asked Claire what she understood me to be saying after one of my "helpful" comments. She flushed and stuttered, "You were explaining how I didn't get it right."

Stunned, I set to exploring with Claire her thoughts about what had been taking place between us. What unfolded was that in Claire's interior, the leading metric for assessing people was "class": is something high class or low class? The rural town of her childhood measured such things meticulously. There were literally railway tracks running through town; those living on one side had less class than those on the other. Claire had lived on the wrong side but had attended a school on the right side. To navigate socially, she became vigilant to what was acceptable, and sensitized to what was rebuffed. In Claire's world, she had to get things right to avoid being outed as low class. This awareness had seeped into the marrow of her bones, as had the belief that at core she was low class. This "truth" about her was a secret hotbed of shame. "I have been keeping myself hidden," she said. "I haven't been honest and direct with you." For her, therapy was a continual see-sawing between confessing blunders of classlessness and being corrected by someone with class.

My inquiry and Claire's openness allowed her to share a certainty she had been harboring for months: she believed I didn't want to see her anymore because I didn't like her as a person. Screwing up her courage she put it point-blank: "Do you want to continue seeing me in psychotherapy?" Without hesitation I answered yes. I liked Claire. I simply had been missing something essential about her. Claire was shocked, but relieved. The psychotherapy process breathed a bit more freely and the rules in Claire's interior loosened enough to allow some reconfiguring.

Bram and Peebles (2014) describe the importance of learning early in the work about a patient's attitude toward receiving help. Claire's case illustrates the understanding that attitude is not always a simple matter. Sometimes it has to be lived out between the two people before it can be seen.

Embodying

In *The Inner Game of Tennis*, Timothy Gallwey (1974) makes an observation apt to psychotherapy:

> Words can only represent actions, ideas and experience. Language is not the action, and at best can only hint at the subtlety and complexity contained in the [action]. Although the construction [of ideas and words]...can be stored in the part of the mind that remembers language, it must be acknowledged that remembering the instruction is not the same as remembering the [action]. (p. 52)

A tennis instructor can offer brilliant verbal observations, and the player can comprehend those words, but words cannot manifest a player's tennis stroke. Only the player's muscles, bones, and tendons moving through the action of the stroke can. Words are like the lights on the floor of the aisle of an airplane, showing the path toward the exit; to reach the exit, the passenger must physically walk to the door.

Changing the world within requires the body's involvement.

The body knows and remembers through its senses. Experience that we see, hear, touch, move through, taste, and smell is experience that we inhabit and thus can live again. We need to translate the disembodied ideas that we offer our patients into tangible experience. When new behaviors, emotions, responses and sensations are practiced to the point of emerging spontaneously without thinking we know they are now embodied.

In medical school, the model for converting ideas into abilities is not cerebral. It is kinesthetic: See one, do one, teach one.

"See One"

Our patients watch us. They pay attention to how we talk to the receptionist, how we laugh with or complain to colleagues, how we treat someone who mistakenly knocks on the door during the psychotherapy session. They notice our plants or our lack of them, their condition, our style of clothes, how careful we are about our furniture, what we choose to put on our walls. Their ears tune in to our off-the-cuff remarks; their eyes fix on our spontaneous facial expressions. In fact, our patients see more of who we are as persons than we may be aware of, and certainly more than we can control.

When they watch and absorb us their mirror neuron systems activate, impelling them to imitate us involuntarily (Iacoboni, 2008). They soak in our manner of being and speaking with them. This is modeling. Modeling is the most potent form of learning.

To put this powerful intervention to use on our patient's behalf we need to learn as much as we can about our own interior so that our implicit messages do not unwittingly contradict what we are telling our patient explicitly. We must embody what we are teaching. Seeking personal therapy ourselves is an efficient way of doing this (Peebles, 1980, 2020). It widens our emotional repertoire, our comfort with unexpected intensity, and our capacity for an emotional intimacy that is simultaneously close and boundaried. Most importantly, it shows us hidden aspects of ourselves, aspects which, if they remained hidden, could seep into the work in damaging ways. For example, there is empirical evidence that angry or manipulative qualities, however veiled in therapists, damage therapeutic alliances (Peebles, 2018). Engaging in our own personal therapy is both opportunity and responsibility.

That being said, our unintended influence on our patients can never be fully mastered. Patients read us with admixtures of accuracy, distortion, and amplification. It is impossible to sustain emotional resilience and balance continuously. We get tired. We unexpectedly get disrupted when our patient presses a tender spot. The information moving back and forth in relationships is messy.

What we can do in the face of this messiness (in addition to personal therapy) is nurture a way of relating that transforms disruption into growth. A consortium of psychologists collaborating over decades spells out methods and benefits of repairing ruptures in therapeutic relationships (Eubanks et al., 2019; Gardner et al., 2020; Lipner et al., 2019; Samstag & Muran, 2019). There are techniques. There are also inner attitudes such as openness, caring interest, and judicious honesty.

Openness is the ability to calm one's reactivity so that we remain receptive even when unsettled. It is the ability to tolerate not-knowing the whats and whys immediately; to remain non-defensive without concluding prematurely.

Caring interest is a joy in connecting and learning. It is being enlivened by new information and embracing the unknown as fascinating rather than threatening. It invites feedback and allows us to hear the truths in our patients' observations about us, while simultaneously contemplating the truths we know about ourselves.

Judicious honesty means recognizing mistakes with honesty. At the same time, honesty and authenticity do not mean sharing everything we know and feel. Judicious honesty appreciates that a therapist's self-disclosure is a volatile ingredient in a therapeutic process. It is to be used with experience, training, and care.

When we invest in these qualities in ourselves, we safeguard and potentiate our patient's vulnerable process of taking us in.

"Do One," Inside Sessions

To "do-one" in psychotherapy starts with the relationship with the therapist. The patient is doing with us what they do with others, so whatever they wish they could change will play out with us and however they would like to be can be practiced with us. Our willingness to be in relationship with our patient provides him a rich laboratory for experimentation.

How we respond depends on what our patient is working on. Elena was tangled by her racing, complex associations. She was working on slowing down her mind so that she could communicate her ideas clearly and garner the caring and respect she yearned for. When she somersaulted through chains of associations with me and ended with, "Do you understand?" and I didn't, I would explain with kindness, "You went pretty fast for me there, and I'm not sure exactly yet what you're wanting me to understand. I understood up to the point where you talked about Martha and then I couldn't follow you after that." Elena might apologize, but I would respond with, "No, no, it's fine, I want to understand. I get glimmers of it. Can you go back over just a little more slowly? I'm sure I'll get it if you do." Through experimenting in real time with me, Elena was learning to identify when her thought processes went too rapidly for listeners and how to recalibrate her thinking and speaking to reach the other person. I conveyed faith in her ability and patience with whatever time it took. Elena's skill in handling the stallion of her processing grew and she said she felt physically more anchored in her body, almost as if her center of gravity had shifted. She was excited about her competence. Both her skill and sensation of substance began emerging naturally with other people, not just with me.

Frida was struggling with the panic that emerged when emotions with no felt shape, name, or words flooded her. Historically she had managed such moments by shutting off sensations and turning to logic. Hesitantly she began trusting herself and me enough to take risks in the sessions with emotion. I maintained eye contact to anchor her. I guided her. "You don't have words. You only have sensations. We'll find the words, a little at a time, by going slowly enough." I held as important any word she found. She held out her hands and wordlessly showed me the tremor of her fingers. "You're trembling inside." She nodded. "You're so afraid that your whole body is trembling." Frida nodded again. Word by word, we pieced together a linguistic scaffolding for her panic. When she broke off, berating herself for being unable to explain I said, "You *are* explaining, in bits and pieces. This is what it looks like, to translate sensations into words. All we have is sensations sometimes. The words come, if we go slowly enough." There were no shortcuts or sudden breakthroughs. Frida needed to feel herself feeling and feel herself being able to find her thinking while she was feeling, one unsure moment at a time.

Role playing is also a form of doing within the therapeutic relationship. When we have never performed behavior we aspire to, and perhaps have not even seen it, our mind is blank about what that behavior looks like. A picture could help. Role playing, with the therapist modeling a rough draft of what the patient's saying or doing something might look like, offers a short movie of new behavior. The patient can take on the role of the other person he anticipates interacting with. This helps his perspective enlarge about how he anticipates the other person might respond. I always ask the patient afterward, "What did you notice? What did that feel like? What struck you the most? What surprised you?" A patient is often fascinated by how non-threatening the words they are afraid to speak actually feel when heard from the viewpoint of a listener. Role playing also allows a patient to identify specific words or messages they are afraid of communicating. This allows us to zero in on details needing exploration and unpacking. Finally, for hands-on learners, role-playing is invaluable because doing an experience is their primary portal for comprehending ideas.

When the patient is playing the other in the scenario and isn't sure what to say, I suggest, "Just make something up." More often than not, what they "make up" is very close to the nature of the person they are portraying. When a patient suddenly becomes silent after several exchanges in the role play and says, "I don't know what she would say next," I respond: "That's good. We're exactly where we want to be. We're somewhere different from what you're used to expecting. That means we're at a place where something new might happen."

Some readers might feel concerned that role-playing shades too easily into "telling" a patient what to do. But for me, role-playing is about brainstorming and storyboarding options together. I always refer to it as "rough drafts," and "let's play with it and see what happens."

Composing emails and texts together is another way to "do" inside the therapy session. How a person writes is how they think. One of my supervisors focused on therapists' write-ups to help clarify where their thinking was fuzzy or inaccurate. Working with a patient's texts and emails in psychotherapy accomplishes something similar. When the patient and I read them together we learn where the confusion or conflict is in the patient's thinking. The patient recognizes the spots of inner uneasiness more clearly when he re-reads what he wrote through my eyes.

Ellen and I often worked through the medium of composing emails and texts to family members and care providers. At first, she and I would discuss an interchange she was trying to have, and I might ask her permission to compose a note on her phone that captured what we were talking about. (Sometimes I think more clearly when I write.) Ellen watched me compose and would use parts or all of it in her texts. As time went on, Ellen brought in her own drafts for me to read, and she listened as I experimented aloud with tweaks to her wording. I asked her how this or that sounded, not with literary intent, but with therapeutic intent of engaging Ellen's senses as she felt the impact of her words on others and the impact inside herself when speaking those words. Eventually, Ellen was writing texts entirely on her own. Through such "doing" Ellen was building capacities: to organize her thinking in orderly ways, to identify when conflict caused her to obfuscate, and to recognize what speaking directly looked like.

There are numerous other ways to bring "doing" into therapy sessions. Entire modalities are built around incorporating the kinesthetic and sensory into psychotherapy in order to access experience that is held in the body rather than in words, and in order to shift affective, cognitive, and behavioral patterns through embodying changes not merely thinking about and deliberating them. We mentioned a few of these earlier (p. 51, this chapter). Jacob Moreno's psychodrama (1980), Fritz Perl's gestalt therapy (Perls et al., 1951), Jay Haley's problem-solving therapy (1987), and Minuchin's structural family therapy (1974) are a few classic examples. The creative arts therapies, Sensorimotor psychotherapy (Ogden & Fisher, 2015), and Somatic Experiencing (Payne et al., 2015) are more recent ones.

"Do One," Outside Sessions

Intentionally practicing expanded ways of relating to one's Self and others each day complexifies the neural networks of our world within, making our interior more flexible and richer in possibilities. Repetition keeps the energy exchange between outer and inner vibrant and helps new neural configurations sustain (see"Monday maps" and "Friday maps," pp. 1–2, this book). No manner of doing or format is too pedestrian or inconsequential. Life lived is a mosaic of tiny details: one thought at a time, one comment restrained at a time, one perception reexamined at a time. Each makes a difference.

Mental rehearsal is vital as well. Most of us run loops of vivid images and sensations from embarrassing social moments over and over in our heads, hoping to purge their sting from our gut. However, by mentally rehearsing such situations we *re-expose* our minds and bodies to reliving them fifty or more times; for example, when we imagine something our visual cortex works just as it does when we are perceiving it (Le Bihan et al., 1993). This etches imprints of shame and negative self-images into our physical self more deeply; i.e., we are strengthening their embodiment. Why not use the same method for amplifying moments of mastery, growth, or joy? We should give what we feel good about at least equal airtime in our minds if not more. The more vivid, detailed, and sensory our mental rehearsal, the greater number of neural networks are activated and interlaced in our brain.

Activities outside therapy can augment and strengthen the therapeutic work. Meditation, guided imagery, sports, judo, yoga, and Feldenkreis are a few examples. Elena took Feldenkreis classes to deepen her physical sensations of slowing down and acquire concrete methods to ground herself, rein in her thoughts, and feel a physically based sensation of mental coherence. Ben meditated and Ellen used yoga, each to grow agency over calming their body's agitation. Evie played weekend soccer as a way of practicing standing her ground as she held fast to something (the soccer ball) that others were aggressively trying to take away, a symbolic experience for her of speaking truth to power. Frida built up her running skills to feel the power of her muscles and a concrete sensation of their ability to help her escape unsafe situations.

"Teach One"

Over time, our patients become their own psychotherapists, teaching and guiding themselves long after formal therapy sessions have ended. They internalize a way of thinking and a style of relating to themselves through the modeling and practicing we've discussed.

To enhance internalization, it helps for therapists to flag patients' changes aloud as they occur in sessions. We discussed this briefly in

Chapter 1 (p. 8, this book). This helps our patients develop the habit of recognizing their own growth and enjoying mastery and competence. As therapists, we hold a mental map of where our patient began, what his goals were, where he is now, and what more is left to do. With that map in mind, it is easy to catch the moments where his growth noticeably consolidates. Highlight these moments for him. Doing so builds perspective, inspires hope, and models a compassionate way of tracking oneself. For example, I said to Ellen, "The way you spoke to your daughter's doctor about your concerns that he was missing her lethargy was organized and direct. You presented yourself with respect for what you were saying and with respect for his skill. Notice how clearly he answered you! That was largely due to your putting your question so clearly!" After Ellen paused to take this in, I added, "Two years ago you wouldn't have been able to do this. Back then you might have jumped from feeling disappointed to believing he was exploiting you. Your anger might have confused you. But yesterday, with him, you were steady and clear. A lot has changed." My marking the change in Ellen explicitly not only helped her notice it. It amplified her appreciating that change in a deeply sensory way. The world-within changes through deeply sensory experiences.

Discouragement

Feeling discouraged in psychotherapy is inevitable. Think about trying to change the posture of your body, even with the help of a physical therapist. Despite practicing diligently, the muscles slump all too easily back to their original positions, particularly when we are tired. To readjust one's physical alignment takes determination and discipline. The same is true for readjusting one's psychological alignment.

Understanding that setbacks and discouragement are natural helps patients and therapists put aside unnecessary worry. A person's reverting to old feelings and old responses is not a cause for alarm. Our focus is on what one does after he falls down, not on the fact that he fell. We don't attack or blame. We understand setbacks as useful signals that the person was tackling too much at that point in time or perhaps was operating under some of the HALT conditions we discussed in Chapter 3. We hold ourselves and help our patients hold themselves as compassionately as we hold our own children when they are growing and learning. I offer my patients the example of an 11-month-old who pulls himself up and "cruises" along the edge of a couch. Inevitably, he plops back down, but he doesn't crumple in despair and conclude he'll never be able to walk. He may look startled, but it's only for a second. Usually he's quickly back up trying again, particularly when Mother is all encouragement and smiles.

When discouragement shadows the work, it is also valuable for therapists and patients to examine expectations of oneself, of therapy, and of life.

We may need to explain to our patients certain realities of being human. We cannot erase memories. What happened will always be a lived reality, a part of our history, there to emerge at times of fatigue or stress. What we *can* do is develop our capacities to select, engage in, and rehearse healthy new experiences, so that over time we accumulate more good experiences in our interior than unfortunate ones. We can strengthen our capacity to stay balanced in our lives and we can deepen our empathy for ourselves. As we practice such capacities and gain experience recovering from setbacks, we become better able to recognize slip-ups as they are occurring or soon after; the slipping backwards occurs less frequently and feels less intense; and we are able to re-find our equilibrium more swiftly.

Finally, with patients who have suffered psychotic breaks, severe depression, mania, or trauma, I find it useful to explain to them that their original terrifying mental states were so consuming that they often qualify as traumatizing in themselves, leaving earmarks of posttraumatic stress disorder (PTSD). More specifically, bodily sensations similar to their original felt loss of control over their mind or mood can trigger fears that they are falling again fast and hard. As with any person with PTSD, it helps to carve out what differentiates the now from the then. Specifically, patients who suffered depression in the past need to learn how to distinguish *depression* from normal fatigue, the low energy of physical illness, and grieving. Patients who suffered manic episodes need to learn how to distinguish *mania* from joyful enlivenment, the agitation of anxiety, and hypomania.

In Chapter 5, we explore ways to develop and strengthen the capacity to stay inside the unknown.

References

Banyai, E., Meszaros, I., & Csokay, L. (1985). Interaction between hypnotist and subject: A social psychophysiologic approach (preliminary report). In D. Waxman, P.C. Misra, M. Gibson, & M.A. Basker (Eds.), *Modern trends in hypnosis* (pp. 97–108). Boston, MA: Springer.

Bateson, G., Jackson, D., Haley, J., & Weakland, J. (1956). Toward a theory of schizophrenia. *Behavioral Science, 1*(4), 251–264.

Bowlby, J. (1969). *Attachment and loss* (Vol. 1). New York, NY: Basic Books.

Bram, A.D., & Peebles, M.J. (2014). *Psychological testing that matters: Creating a road map for effective treatment.* Washington, DC: American Psychological Association.

Erickson, M.H. (1964/1980). The confusion technique in hypnosis. In E.L. Rossi (Ed.) *The collected papers of Milton H. Erickson on hypnosis: Vol. 1: The nature of hypnosis and suggestion* (pp. 258–291). New York: Irvington.

Erikson, E. (1957/1964). The nature of clinical evidence. In *Insight and responsibility* (pp. 47–80). New York, NY: W.W. Norton & Company.

Eubanks, C.F., Muran, J.C., & Safran, J.D. (2019). Repairing alliance ruptures. In J.C. Norcross & M.J. Lambert (Eds.), *Psychotherapy relationships that* work: *Evidence-based therapist contributions* (3rd ed., Vol. 1, pp. 549–579). New York, NY: Oxford University Press.

Feldenkrais, M. (1985). *The potent self: A study of spontaneity and compulsion.* Berkeley, CA: Frog, Ltd. and Somatic Resources.

Feldenkrais, M. (2019). *The elusive obvious: The convergence of movement, neuroplasticity and health.* Berkeley CA: North Atlantic Books and Somatic Resources.

Fonagy, P., Gergely, G., Jurist, E., & Target, M. (2002). *Affect regulation, mentalization, and the development of the self.* London, UK: Routledge.

Gallwey, W.T. (1974). The inner game of tennis. New York, NY: Random House.

Gardner, J.R., Lipner, L.M., Eubanks, C.F., & Muran, J.C. (2020). A therapist's guide to repairing ruptures in the working alliance. In J.N. Fuertes (Ed.), *Working alliance skills for mental health professionals* (pp. 159–180). New York, NY: Oxford University Press.

Geller, S., & Porges, S.W. (2014). Therapeutic presence: Neurophysiological mechanisms mediating feeling safe in therapeutic relationships. *Journal of Psychotherapy Integration, 24*(3), 178–192.

Goldberg, S., Muir, R., & Kerr, J. (Eds.). (1995). *Attachment theory: Social, developmental, and clinical perspectives.* Hillsdale, NJ: The Analytic Press.

Haley, J. (1987). *Problem-solving therapy.* San Francisco, CA: Jossey-Bass.

Hasson, U., Ghazanfar, A.A., Galantucci, B., Garrod, S., & Keysers, C. (2012). Brain-to-brain coupling: A mechanism for creating and sharing a social world. *Trends in Cognitive Sciences, 16*(2), 114–121.

Holzer, J. (1989). Selections From the Living Series [sculpture]. Minneapolis Sculpture Garden, Walker Art Center. Minneapolis, MN. (c) 2021 Jenny Holzer, member Artists Rights Society (ARS), New York.

Horwitz, L. (1983). Projective identification in dyads and groups. *International Journal of Group Psychotherapy, 33*(3), 259–279.

Iacoboni, M. (2008). *Mirroring people: The science of empathy and how we connect with others.* New York, NY: Farrar, Straus and Giroux.

Kahneman, D. (2011). *Thinking, fast and slow.* New York, NY: Farrar, Straus and Giroux.

Le Bihan, D., Turner, R., Zeffiro, T.A., Cuenod, C.A., Jezzard, P., & Bonnerot, V. (1993). Activation of human primary visual cortex during visual recall: A magnetic resonance imaging study. *Proceedings National Academy of Sciences, 90*(24), 11802–11805.

Lehrner, A., & Yehuda, R. (2018). Cultural trauma and epigenetic inheritance. *Development and Psychopathology, 30*(5), 1763–1777.

Linton, P.H., Travis, R.P., Kuechenmeister, C.A., & White, H. (1977). Correlation between heart rate covariation, personality and hypnotic state. *American Journal of Clinical Hypnosis, 19*(3), 148–154.

Lipner, L.M., Liu, D., & Muran, J.C. (2019). Getting on the same page: Introducing alliance rupture as a path to mutual empathy and change in psychotherapy. In A. Foster & Z. Yaseen (Eds.), *Teaching empathy in healthcare* (pp. 117–126). Cham, Switzerland: Springer.

McCraty, R., Atkinson, M., Tomasino, D., & Tiller, W.A. (1998). The electricity of touch: Detection and measurement of cardiac energy exchange between people. In K. Pribram (Ed.), *Brain and values: Is a biological science of values possible?* (pp. 359–379). Mahwah, NJ: Lawrence Erlbaum Associates.

McCraty, R., Rozman, D., & Childre, D. (1999). *HeartMath: A new biobehavioral intervention for increasing health and personal effectiveness.* Amsterdam, NL: Harwood Academic Publishers.

McGilchrist, I. (2009). *The master and his emissary.* New Haven, CT: Yale University Press.

Minuchin, S. (1974). *Families and family therapy.* Cambridge, MA: Harvard University Press.

Moreno, J.L. (1980), *Psychodrama* (Vol I, II & III). Beacon, NY: Beacon House Inc.

Ogden, P., & Fisher, J. (2015). *Sensorimotor psychotherapy: Interventions for trauma and attachment.* New York, NY: W.W. Norton.

Ogden, P., Minton, K., & Pain, C. (2006). *Trauma and the body: A sensorimotor approach to psychotherapy.* New York, NY: W.W. Norton.

Otani, A. (1989). The confusion technique untangled: Its theoretical rationale and preliminary classification. *American Journal of Clinical Hypnosis, 31*(3), 164–172.

Payne, P., Levine, P.A., & Crane-Godreau, M.A. (2015). Somatic experiencing: Using interception and proprioception as core elements of trauma therapy. *Frontiers in Psychology, 6*(Article 93), 1–18.

Peebles, M.J. (1980). Personal therapy and the ability to display empathy, warmth and genuineness in psychotherapy. *Psychotherapy: Theory, Research and Practice, 17,* 258–262.

Peebles, M.J. (2012). *Beginnings: The art and science of planning psychotherapy* (2nd ed.). New York, NY: Routledge Press.

Peebles, M.J. (2018). Harm in hypnosis: Three understandings from psychoanalysis that can help. *American Journal of Clinical Hypnosis, 60*(3): 239–261.

Peebles, M.J. (2020). Longing and fear: The ambivalence about having a relationship in psychotherapy. *American Journal of Clinical Hypnosis, 62*(1–2), 138–158.

Peebles-Kleiger, M.J. (1989). Using countertransference in the hypnosis of trauma victims: Hazards that can facilitate healing. *American Journal of Psychotherapy, 43*(4), 518–530.

Perls, F., Hefferline, G., & Goodman, P. (1951). *Gestalt therapy: Excitement and growth in the human personality.* New York, NY: Delta Book.

Pikovsky, A., Rosenblum, M., & Kurths, J. (2001). *Synchronization: A universal concept in nonlinear sciences.* Cambridge, UK: Cambridge University Press.

Racker, H. (1957). The meanings and uses of countertransference. *Psychoanalytic Quarterly, 26*(3), 303–357.

Reich, W. (1945). *Character analysis* (3rd ed.). New York, NY: Farrar, Straus and Giroux.

Rosenthal, R., & Jacobson, L. (1968). *Pygmalion in the classroom: Teacher expectations and pupils' intellectual development.* New York, NY: Holt, Rinehart & Winston.

Rudin, S., Niccol, A., Feldman, E.S., & Schroeder, A. (Producers), & Weir, P. (Director). (1998). *The Truman show.* [Motion picture]. United States: Paramount Pictures.

Russek, L., & Schwartz, G. (1994). Interpersonal heart-brain registration and the perception of parental love: A 42 year follow-up of the Harvard Mastery of Stress Study. *Subtle Energies, 5*(3), 195–208.

Samstag, L.W., & Muran, J.C. (2019). Ruptures, repairs, and reflections: Contributions of Jeremy Safran. *Research in Psychotherapy: Psychopathology, Process and Outcome, 22*(1), 7–14.

Schafer, R. (1958). How was this story told? *Journal of Projective Techniques, 22*(2), 181–210

Schore, A.N. (1994). *Affect regulation and the origin of the self: Neurobiology of emotional development.* Hillsdale, NJ: Lawrence Erlbaum Associates, Publishers.

Schore, A.N. (2009). Right-brain affect regulation: An essential mechanism of development, trauma, dissociation, and psychotherapy. In D. Fosha, D.J. Siegel, & M. Solomon (Eds.), *The healing power of emotion: Affective neuroscience, development, and clinical practice* (pp. 112–144). New York, NY: W.W. Norton & Company.

Shectman, F., & Harty, M.K. (1986). Treatment implications of object relationships as they unfold during the diagnostic interaction. In M. Kissen (Ed.), *Assessing object relations phenomena* (pp. 279–303). New York, NY: International Universities Press.

Spitz, R.A. (1945). Hospitalism: An inquiry into the genesis of psychiatric conditions in early childhood. *Psychoanalytic Study of the Child, 1*(1), 53–74.

Stern, D. (1985). *The interpersonal world of the infant: A view from psychoanalysis and developmental psychology.* New York, NY: Basic Books.

Tippett, K. (Host). (2017, October 5). Daniel Kahneman: Why we contradict ourselves and confound each other [Audio podcast]. In *On being with Krista Tippett.* WNYC Studios. https://onbeing.org/programs/daniel-kahneman-why-we-contradict-ourselves-and-confound-each-other-jan2019/

UMass Boston. (2009, November 30). Still face experiment: Dr. Edward Tronick [Video file]. Youtube. https://www.youtube.com/watch?v=apzXGEbZht0

Westen, D. (2007). *The political brain: The role of emotion in deciding the fate of the nation.* New York, NY: Public Affairs.

Woldt, A.L., & Toman, S.M. (2005). *Gestalt therapy: History, theory, and practice.* Thousand Oaks, CA: Sage Publications, Inc.

Yapko, M. (1999). *Hand-me-down blues: How to stop depression from spreading in families.* New York, NY: St. Martin's Press.

Yehuda, R., Lehrner, A., & Bierer, L.M. (2018). The public reception of putative epigenetic mechanisms in the transgenerational effects of trauma. *Environmental Epigenetics, 4*(2), 1–7.

5   Learning to Not-Know

The only point of importance in any session is the unknown.
—Wilfred Bion, Notes On Memory and Desire

In the 1960s, Elizabeth Zetzel (1965) wrote an essay that turned ideas about depression upside down. Instead of describing depression as something toxic to be eliminated, she spoke of a capacity—the capacity to *bear* depression. She saw this capacity as a sign of strength and maturity. She encouraged surrendering to depression's disquietude in order to actively ponder what it might be trying to tell us. Emmy Gut (1982) went further. She saw depression as a basic human emotion, neither "good or bad, healthy or sick in itself" (p. 180). In fact, she considered depression to be potentially adaptive, with "the potential to serve a vital function" (p. 180). As Gut saw it, depression was a pathway to creative thinking and alternative solutions. If one listens to depression as a signal and does not smother or fight it, accepts the slowed down feeling, cuts back on activities accordingly and decreases extraneous demands on the mind, one is freed to identify sources of the disequilibrium and transform them. Gut saw this as "productive depression," when "some useful learning or maturation has occurred, some behavior been reorganized, some plan revised so that...we function more effectively in the attainment of some goal" (p. 180).

Our unease with not-knowing deserves a similar recalibration. Saying, "I don't know," is an *ability*. It requires a mature self-esteem, mental flexibility, and openness to learning. When psychotherapy feels stuck, a therapist's being able to say, "I don't know what to do right now," or, "I don't know why this isn't working," breathes life back into the process. It is tempting to grab hold of incomplete and premature conclusions when we feel lost. But staying inside an experience of not-knowing becomes a doorway to creative thinking.

Bion (1967/2013) points out that in psychotherapy the unknown is the only place of importance. It is only inside the unknown that new answers

DOI: 10.4324/9781315449043-5

and new possibilities lie. But Kahneman (2011) explains that humans are driven to want answers so that not-knowing can feel intolerable at times to patient and therapist alike: "[There is] a puzzling limitation of our mind: our excessive confidence in what we believe we know; and our apparent inability to acknowledge the full extent of our ignorance and the uncertainty of the world we live in" (pp. 13–14). This chapter talks about the drawbacks in psychotherapy of trying too hard to-know, ways to understand the felt threats of not-knowing, and methods of cultivating this useful capacity in ourselves and in our patients.

We Are Wired to Want to Know

Being able to not-know is not easy. We are wired to detect patterns in order to function efficiently. For example, we wouldn't want our nightly commute to be new each time we navigated it. Our mind's energy is better spent putting that route on automatic and using those 20 minutes to figure out what to eat for dinner instead.

Detecting patterns also keeps us safe. For example, Frida learned to choose her words carefully when speaking with her father. She knew he had a pattern of erupting violently if someone implied that he was less than perfect. Frida didn't have the luxury of not-knowing. She needed to predict father's response; the consequences of not doing so were emotionally dire. Seeing the pattern of her father's behavior was survival.

We are unconsciously drawn to people who promise answers and seem certain about their perceptiveness. We look to them as leaders and are willing to follow where they point. Our patients look to us similarly. They hope that we will know, and their wish can hook us internally into leaping prematurely into proclamations that, if we are being honest with ourselves, have little basis in data or facts.

Groopman (2007) cautions us about such leaps. He points out the dangers of certainty in medical diagnoses. When we feel pressured into certainty, we fail to look for discontinuities and exceptions. We don't push ourselves to think outside our mental boxes and search for what we might not be considering; instead, we look for data that confirm what we initially see. Gladwell (2005) illustrates how emotional arousal plus time pressure erode the accuracy of our perceptions even further. When our heart rate speeds up and time is short, facts give way to stereotypes. Fatal mistakes can be made, as when Amadou Diallo, an innocent man, was shot dead by four policemen in the Bronx in 1999 (Gladwell, 2005). Kahneman (2011) supports both Groopman's and Gladwell's observations with experimental data: humans gravitate toward thinking that is swift and effortless to thinking that takes time and the discipline to look longer. In short, an evolutionary asset—detecting patterns—turns into a liability under conditions of certainty, emotional arousal, and time pressure.

The Illusion of "Knowing"

Not everything can be known. When humans, emotions, and relationships are involved, we speak of probabilities, not certainty. The possible combinations of factors in play are infinite. There are always elements we don't even know to consider and can't identify in retrospect. Think about the 2016 United States presidential election. Every poll and pundit predicted with statistically-based confidence that Hilary Clinton would win. At the time of this writing, intelligent people are still deliberating over what was not measured, what was not asked, and what was never considered to make this prediction so wrong.

It is difficult for the human mind to wrap itself around, much less accept, that, "The more we discover, the more we understand that what we don't yet know is greater than what we know" (Rovelli, 2017, p. 6). Even more bewildering is that it is impossible to know what we don't know. (Magee (2016) points out:

> The already-visible universe is 1,000,000,000,000,000,000,000,000 miles across. The Astronomer Royal tells us that we must expect the not-yet-visible universe to extend beyond that by distances which—measured not in miles but in light-years—would be written 'not with ten zeros, not even with a hundred, but with millions'...Reality will never be intellectually mastered by humans....This is not...to say we cannot understand anything. But it is certainly to say that we cannot understand everything...Most of reality is unknowable by us, and—because beyond all possibility of apprehension—unconceptualisable. (pp. 8, 15, 16, 85)

Rovelli (2017), a 21st-century physicist, alludes to Plato and his Allegory of the Cave when he writes, "We are all in the depths of a cave, chained by our ignorance, by our prejudices, and our weak senses reveal to us only shadows. If we try to see further, we are confused" (p. 8).

So when a patient says, "I know *exactly* what she'll say!" or, "I know what's going to happen," I respond, "How?" I understand that my patient's ability to tolerate not-knowing is a capacity we will need to work on, but I ask anyway, to plant seeds of doubt in her mind about her certainty when it comes to predicting the future.

Why is it vital in psychotherapy to challenge such certainties?

For one thing, predictions about behavior and the future are circular. Since we predict from inside a world of what we know, we are doing little more than assuming that what has happened to us in the past will be the same thing that is going to happen in the future. Usually, we're oblivious that we're building our predictions on an idiosyncratic sample set; in fact, we derive a false sense of security from our circular reasoning. We tell ourselves some version of, "I recognize exactly what's going on! This person is Type X. I've been with this type before and here is what he is going to do!" But, as Daniel Kahneman (2011) points out, such thinking is a notorious source of human error. Kahneman names this the WYSIATI error ("What you see is all [you think] there is") (p. 88). He explains that what makes this error insidious is that it is regularly accompanied by—here it is again—a profound sense of confidence in its rightness.

Even worse, decades of social psychological research demonstrate that expecting a particular outcome increases the likelihood of its happening (Rosenthal & Jacobson, 1968). This "expectation effect" is so ubiquitous and powerful that its discovery changed the standard for scientific research design (Rosenthal, 1966; 1976). Prior to the confirmation of the expectation effect, research assistants running experiments knew what a study's hypotheses were, which outcomes would confirm those hypotheses, and to which experimental group their current subjects were assigned. Such knowledge was enough to regularly influence results toward confirming the researchers' hypotheses, even when the subjects were rats! (As a result, keeping both the experimental assistants and the subjects in the dark about the outcomes being sought and the groups they were in ["double-blind"] became a requirement for credible empirical research [Rosenthal, 1976]).

There is a certain kind of accurate "knowing" without knowing how we know (Mayer, 2007; McGilchrist, 2009). People call this intuition or a gut-feeling. While intuition can be right, it can also be wrong. Sometimes our gut's "knowing" emerges from wishes and fears rather than from the facts in front of us. People look but they cannot always see. They hear but they may not be listening. Speed, emotional arousal, and certainty blur accuracy: "I thought I saw a gun in his hand...What I seen was an entire weapon. A square weapon in his hand," testified Officer Ken Boss after the killing of Amadou Diallo (Gladwell, 2005, p. 193). Diallo had been holding his wallet, not a gun.

The Power of Uncertainty

Un-certainty helps slow us down.

If we can tolerate being uncertain, everything stills. We listen differently. We don't feel a need to tumble over our patient's words imagining we know where her thoughts are leading. We don't feel pressured to have an answer in our head when she hasn't yet finished her sentence. Instead, we understand that we *cannot* know what to say next until we fully hear what she is saying now. We cannot fully hear what she is saying now unless we also give her additional time to hear the words she just spoke and to notice how it feels to have said them aloud. In those spaces of waiting, our minds resonate with feelings, images, and remembered bits of conversations as well, which are also part of the communication taking place. This is how thoughtful conversation unfolds. It is not pre-scripted. The advantage to such thoughtfulness is that when we don't prematurely fill in our patient's unfinished phrases with what we think she might be meaning, the gaps in our patient's thinking emerge. These gaps include missing details, contradictions, and confusing explanations. They are important because they signal places that our patient is hiding from herself, doesn't understand, is conflicted about, or hasn't translated into words. When we let these gaps emerge, we are able to ask about them.

Uncertainty, with curiosity and without shame, opens walls of compartmented thinking as well. Else Frenkel-Brunswik (1949) called this ability a "tolerance of ambiguity." It is associated with flexibility and creativity, the ability to enjoy nuances, and the capacity to allow contradictory information to be considered rather than rejected. It is associated with appreciating that there may be more than one solution to a given puzzle, with enjoying complexity, and with being unafraid of novelty. These are all change-friendly traits.

When therapists are able to tolerate uncertainty, the therapeutic alliance strengthens. Groopman (2007) writes:

> Taking uncertainty into account can enhance a physician's therapeutic effectiveness, because it demonstrates his honesty, his willingness to be more engaged with his patients, his commitment to the reality of the situation...And it makes it easier for the doctor to change course if the first strategy fails, to keep trying. Uncertainty sometimes is essential for success. (p. 155)

Being honest about one's uncertainty reinforces partnership rather than hierarchy. The patient is galvanized into thinking *with* us rather than nodding passively to whatever we say. Some patients are relieved when I admit I don't know yet what to do. When I share this without worry or self-blame, they feel less afraid, foolish, or wrong for not knowing what to do themselves. I explain that sometimes in therapy we just have to sit, not-knowing together what something means or what to do and see what emerges next. Doing so can be a profoundly therapeutic experience for a patient. For some, it is the first time they have felt not-alone in feeling lost in their inner darkness. When we are straightforward about not-knowing, our patient is more likely to trust us when we do know.

Uncertainty helps prevent us from repeating mistakes. Researchers learned to stay blind to the hypothesized outcome of their subjects' activities in order to prevent self-fulfilling prophecies. We would do well to take a page from that method. To make something "different" possible, we must be able to resist concluding that what has always happened will keep on happening. Developing the ability to not-know helps us do this.

Even Bill Murray, the grumpy weatherman, Phil, in *Groundhog Day*, recognized this to be true:

Phil: Something is...different.
Rita: Good or bad?
Phil: Anything different is good.

Uncertainty is also reality. It is the reality of living life as a human in this universe. McGilchrist (2009) writes:

> Niels Bohr's 'Copenhagen interpretation' of quantum mechanics and Werner Heisenberg's Uncertainty Principle established a universe in which uncertainty is at the core, not just a product of human imperfection, to be remedied in time by advances in learning, but in the very nature of things. (p. 136)

In Western culture, it is normal to try to wrestle uncertainty to the ground. With our can-do attitude, we look around, see things not working out the way people wanted, vow this won't happen to us, and tell ourselves anything is possible given a good plan and the right effort. We deny uncertainty by committing to a set of rules that promise control over outcome; e.g., "If I work hard I will be noticed at work and rewarded." We try to eliminate uncertainty by ignoring information that contradicts our assumptions, makes our view of things more complicated than we want, and makes us feel uneasy. We try to outsmart uncertainty by researching "to the ends of the internet." We try to outpace uncertainty's anxiety by plunging into races for recognition, influence, power, and acquisition. Such efforts to deny, eliminate, and outsmart uncertainty are futile in the long run. They are futile because they offer no method for dealing straightforwardly with the inevitable limitations we eventually face in terms of intelligence, forethought, ability to influence outcomes, or the capacity to rebound physically and mentally from setbacks in the idealized ways we wish would happen. In contrast, learning how to feel uncertain or unable and still feel intact, steady, and generative builds a strength that flows from being capable of dealing with reality rather than a false confidence that flows from believing we can bend reality. This is the source of true resilience.

Allowing uncertainty is not the same as being unable to make a decision; it opens room for imagining alternatives we have not thought of before. It quiets the noise of presumptions so that we can hear contradictions, entertain doubts and questions, and spark wondering. It helps us come to fuller, more creative decisions.

Being able to not-know is not the same as having no knowledge. It is being humble about the limits of our knowledge. Humility is the child of self-assuredness. "Humility is an important psychological strength...

A person who experiences humility is likely to have an accurate assessment of his or her own accomplishments and abilities...which might result from the increased, non-defensive self-insight that is associated with high cognitive complexity" (King & Hicks, 2007, p. 632). Being able to not-know allows us to ask what we might *not* be seeing, whether because we never learned it, because our field has not considered it, or because we were taught that it was "wrong."

The pressure to-know can be contagious in a psychotherapy session. It is up to us to interrupt it.

Developing the Skill of Not-Knowing

> Anything that is interesting is messy. And the converse is true as well.
>
> —Paul Pruyser, *personal communication*, October 19, 1984

To develop the capacity for not-knowing, we must enjoy complexity. We must be willing to muck about in messy places.

Gladwell (2008) described a young, 20-something nurse, Renee, who was playing with a computer program at the behest of Stanford mathematician, Alan Schoenfeld. Schoenfeld was interested in how people solve problems, but Renee didn't know this. All she knew was she was trying to figure out which numbers to plug in to make a vertical line cross the x-axis. Renee wasn't particularly skilled with numbers, but what she did have was an unusual ability to experiment and puzzle over something that she did not know. She never attacked herself or gave up. She wasn't driven in an anxious way. She was simply curious and interested. She had a "willingness to work hard for 22 minutes to make sense of something" (p. 246). When she discovered the answer—and it was discovery in the true sense of the word—her face lit up. "Ahhhh. That means something now. I won't forget that!" (p. 244). This is what we wish for our patients: discoveries that they won't forget.

Being comfortable with not having an answer, enough so that we are able to puzzle and explore for stretches of time, is an ability that can be grown. Recognizing the pressure to-know, being willing to be vulnerable, shifting fear into curiosity, and practicing are core ingredients for developing this skill.

Naming the Pressure To-Know

We can't help predicting. It is our left hemispheric thinking taking over: managing reality by categorizing, systematizing, listing, and feeling in control. This type of processing has its place, but when we feel threatened it over-activates. It propels us into scrabbling to know everything that needs to be known about a specific situation and believing that it is all knowable. We think this makes us safe. Nothing could be further from the truth.

As counterintuitive as it feels, when one feels threatened, safety lies inside calmly *not*-knowing. Quieting ourselves lets us open our eyes to watch, wait, and learn which details emerge as meaningful.

It may be an odd leap when examining psychotherapy, but consider movie depictions of a marksman at work, such as *American Sniper* (Eastwood, 2014). Despite being under heightened threat, a marksman's movements are deliberately slow and methodical. His body may be alert but it is still, not tense. His eye peers through the scope and he waits patiently for the optimal moment to press on the trigger. Even when enemy forces are closing in, he breathes slowly and moves with studied intention to exit in a manner that optimizes his safety.

We can learn from the marksman's mindful patience as he sits inside an uncertain, unknown space. We want to become familiar with our physical cues that our mind and body have begun racing. Common indicators that we are speeding up include talking rapidly, concluding with certainty, and over-planning for what hasn't happened. These behaviors usually roll in so seamlessly that we don't realize at first that they are there.

We met Andrea in Chapter 2. Change threatens Andrea because of its unknowns. She is afraid of being startled, swamped, or knocked off her feet by anything unanticipated that she hadn't prepared for. In response, she developed a method of handling upcoming change, be it change brought on by children's schedules, developmental milestones, her work demands, career shifts, or vacations. Andrea is adept at internet research, so she leaps onto her laptop and tracks down all recommended fixes and options for responding to the anticipated issue. For example, she may research doctors' and parents' opinions for the best age at which to begin toilet training or kindergarten, the best methods and books for preparing the child, the best equipment to use, and the signs and symptoms that the child is not thriving. Andrea's concentration, the breadth of material she covers, and the speed at which she does so are breathtaking. Her method more or less works the more finite the recommended options and the more consensus—or as she would name it, "right answers"—exists. When an objective right or wrong is less definitive and choosing the best path requires feeling into a situation intuitively, Andrea becomes rattled. In a session in which she is rattled, her words rush like a torrent let loose when the sluice of a dam opens. She lists all the options flowing from all possibilities, classifying their pros and cons, only a solution never emerges because for every pro she finds a con. Suddenly she asks, "What should I do?" I invariably startle. My mind has been spinning trying to keep up with her reasoning. To buy time I might ask, "What are you feeling just now?" But Andrea presses, "I don't know. I just need some tools from you to figure this out. Can you give me some?"

Andrea's sudden demand for something concrete in the midst of her distress of floundering usually trips me off-balance. I feel disoriented and inadequate, my mind gone blank. Reflexively I may try to bolster myself by telling myself that I do have more skills for Andrea! However, when I rush to offer such skills and tips to Andrea, who is desperate about not-knowing, her responses are, "I've already tried that," "It doesn't work," or "It won't work." Without realizing it, I became caught up in trying to "know" too. Andrea's rejection of my options aptly signals that I missed the point.

What becomes productive at such moments is to name for myself how unsure I feel. I *don't know* what to tell Andrea—this is a fact—and it makes me nervous. I breathe slowly and let myself become interested rather than afraid. Doing this takes a few seconds but those seconds are enough to open a window through which to *see* Andrea rather than react to her. I notice how my physical feelings of tension and inadequacy are my body's way of empathizing with Andrea's agitation. I notice how my jump-to reflex of offering her solutions is responding to her way of framing the dilemma: if someone knows then we are safe.

I take a few breaths, hold eye contact with Andrea and say, "You're scared about not knowing what to do." I use my understanding of *my* feeling to name her feeling. Tears well in Andrea's eyes, and just when I see her words on the edge of rushing out again, I speak.

"Let me interrupt for a second now if that's ok. I think what would be helpful right now is to just...slow...down and feel...what you're feeling...inside...rather than race with your words. Feel *me here with you* feeling what you're feeling...with you." I breathe slowly, using the pace of my speaking (with pauses indicated by the ellipses in the quote above) as an intervention to shift the pace of her heart rate and breathing. I want to redirect the dynamic of our escalating contagion, from my mirroring her internal state to her mirroring mine.

The first time Andrea and I did this together, she calmed for half a second and then sped up again; her instinctive need to grasp control compelled her. I moved in, gently interrupted, and pulled her back into the slowing. I did this as many times as Andrea needed for her to become less afraid of, and more accustomed to, sitting with the discomfort of not-knowing. It is a little like learning to float. Lying back and letting go into water does not make sense. How can water hold us up? Everything about that sensation tells our body to brace, but the more our muscles try to hold us in place, the faster we sink. It confounds us that letting go completely into liquid is the only way for that liquid to carry us. We only learn to trust this truth once we experience it and repeat it. The same holds true for learning how to float inside the unknown.

As Andrea calmed enough to take in ideas, I named more of what was taking place. "When you don't know what to do, fear grips you, and all you've known to do with that fear is beat it back by getting the 'best' answers. You end up overwhelmed and you still feel lost. When you slow down instead, your brain hears information from inside you. You're able to connect with yourself and feel your priorities and what's important to you. Your mind clears. You focus."

A few years later in our process, Andrea was struggling with a career choice. She moaned, "Everyone says to trust my gut but I don't know what a gut feeling is. I don't have feelings from my gut." This was interesting. I noticed how swiftly my own body mirrored Andrea's. For a nano-second my insides lurched with something like, "Oh no! If she has no gut feelings, what are we going to do??" I was able to notice my physical reaction with interest, settle myself, and mull Andrea's words with curiosity instead of fluster. I waited for what emerged next.

Andrea had learned to be reflective in our silences. After a beat she spoke. "If I don't take this position, I'll regret that I never tried." I let the quality of her voice, her body posture, her eye gaze, and her pace soak into me. When my words caught up to what I was processing, I spoke.

"This is what speaking from your gut feels like. Notice your voice. It's slowed down. The pitch is lower. Your body is calmer. The muscles on your face have loosened and settled. Your body is more relaxed. Can you feel that? Can you hear the difference in your voice?" Andrea did. Within minutes she found her decision.

There are qualitative differences between the information obtained from our left-hemispheric approach of ferreting out and drilling into external data and our right-hemispheric approach of listening for and allowing internal data to emerge spontaneously. It is the holding of the two simultaneously that forms a creative moment. Because Andrea had learned how to become still when she didn't know, she was able to hear the information arising from within her, which breathed meaning into and gave form to the external facts she had assembled. Integrating the two created an organic response that felt satisfying and complete to Andrea. She was still a little scared about her decision, but now she was excited too.

Learning to not-know begins with identifying the pressure to know. Next, we strengthen our ability to be vulnerable.

The Willingness To Be Vulnerable

Not-knowing does not feel good at first. It feels scary, as if filled with unseen and unseeable threats. Medieval maps understood this; they labeled uncharted waters: "Here be dragons." We experience the unknown in our lives as a darkness, and when we peer into it, we imagine outlines of dreads from our past, like children who imagine monsters lurking in the crack of a half-open closet door at night.

Inner dragons and monsters come in all shapes. For Ellen the monster she imagined when she didn't know what someone was thinking was her grandmother's wagging finger and cutting critique. For Ben it was emotional coldness and isolation. For Claire it was being physically small and feeling dominated. In the beginning of therapy, neither Ellen, Ben, nor Claire were able to recognize when they *did not know* another person's motivations during a conversation; each of them concluded that they *did* know. Their prophecies of criticism, isolation, and domination sadly made for self-fulfilling interactions.

The more childhood monsters in one's past, and the more frightening those childhood monsters are, the more difficulty that child-turned-adult has with tolerating uncertainty. Frenkel-Brunswik (1949) saw evidence that childhood homes with chaos, threatening parents who required submission, and arbitrary and overwhelming discipline created children who had difficulty with ambiguity. In those children's lives, one mis-read cue or misstep could turn an ambiguous situation into a bad situation. As adults, they tended toward swift conclusions, absolutes (good/bad, clean/ dirty), and rigidity of views in order to shut down uncertainty. In psychotherapy, such persons press for fast answers or they become anxious or irritable. Their demand for quick certainty is their protection against the vulnerability in not-knowing.

We want to help our patients develop a capacity to feel vulnerable without panicking. They need this capacity so that they can resist jumping to conclusions before they have all the information. When feeling vulnerable is infiltrated with poorly named sensations of threat, it helps to identify the circumstances that originated such sensations. This is the work we talked about in Chapter 4. When we name the threats stalking our inner world, we shrink their power to rule us and increase our power to perceive the outer world more accurately. This is much to our advantage because what is taking place in the outer world usually contains alternatives to our past.

It is important as well to remember the power of language choices (Chapter 2) when expanding a patient's ability to not-know. Patients describe feeling "helpless" when they don't-know; even though they are actively sitting with difficult images, describing them, and opening up to alternative explanations. It is important to name their "stamina" and "competence" as well so that patients can grow a fuller experience of their actual capabilities.

Patients also report feeling scared. We want to empathize with "scared," but also introduce words such as unsettled, disrupted, or uneasy as new ways to conceptualize what they are feeling. By doing so, we nuance their vocabulary for sensations that were originally given a single negative label. They may describe their mind as feeling blank, dark, or empty when they don't-know, implying threat. We can point out that a "blank" feeling is actually neutral. That neutrality of blankness could be equally understood as time to learn, as a place for discovery, and as an opportunity for new possibilities. Doing so paves the way for welcoming the unknown with interest and gratitude. Finally, patients report feeling vulnerable inside an unknown experience. We can direct their attention to how they are actually *choosing* to be open to new perceptions for all the reasons that brought them to therapy. Their choice and their openness reflect the growth that has taken place inside them as a result of their hard work. All such interventions converge on helping our patients replace their automatic and narrow assumptions of threat with awareness of their mastery, choice, and perseverance.

In addition to the vulnerability of feeling afraid and threatened, not-knowing brings the vulnerability of feeling lost. We are relinquishing our go-to reference points. It is unmooring. Harlem (2010) speaks to the uneasiness of feeling-in-exile, "the space between leaving and arriving" (p. 461). This is a space in which we are in-between what feels familiar to us and what feels so unfamiliar that we can't picture it. In this space, patients feel "in between" versions of themselves—the Self with whom they are familiar and the Self who is developing. One patient described this place as being like "white space." Another described it as like being suspended in the middle of a *Star Trek* Transporter process, dematerialized but not yet clearly rematerialized. To add to the queasiness such a vulnerable experience of in-betweenness brings, time feels endless in that place of feeling lost. When we are driving to a new destination in the dark, getting there can feel like it's taking forever. Along the way, we become uncertain: have we taken a wrong turn, missed a signpost, or followed directions that are not right? When we arrive, relief washes over us as we see recognizable lights. We are always surprised at how much shorter the drive back home is. It isn't really shorter; it just feels that way because now we know where we are going.

"Lost" can also refer to the disorientation a person feels when she steps away from an accustomed role she has fulfilled inside her social system. Families of origin, marriage, work, and friendships all form webs of connections. These are eco-systems of energy. When we choose to not to respond as expected, we disrupt a flow of connections. To step outside an accustomed role is to break with our system as it's been functioning, which breaks with the identity and affirmations the role within our system has brought us.

It takes courage to suspend assumptions about ourselves and other people and to allow ourselves to feel uncertain about how they will react and what we will feel. When we suspend assumptions, we need something to hold onto. That something is our connection with our sensory self, our body, as solid, present, existing, and continuous. It is also our connection with a developed confidence that whatever happens we will be able to pause, notice, track, and find a response. That something is as well our connecting and re-connecting in our minds with lived experiences of people who believe us, believe in us, and remain constant, even if at first that is only the therapist. Such touchstones hold our subjective molecules of Self intact as we move through the in-between space from what we have known to what is unknown, bridging older and newer versions of ourselves.

I am reminded of Jonas in *The Giver* (Lowry, 1993), who could not accept the bleakness of his colorless society. To feel fully alive, he had to leave, even though the land beyond his community's perimeters was unknown. Jonas crafts a plan, much like Truman whom we met in Chapter 4 did, to escape. His journey is arduous ("The forests beside the road were dark and thick with mystery" [p. 171]), yet he is propelled by the belief that something more lies ahead. Lowry gives us no certainty in the end; the reader is left with possibility about Jonas' future but no clear known. All that is clear is Jonas' awareness that if he had stayed in his community, "He would have lived a life hungry for feelings, for color, for love" (p. 174).

Jonas' tale captures the feel of what it takes to venture beyond the confines of what one has known, into what is neither familiar nor predictable. We are asking a lot of our patients when we ask them to slow down, pause, and not conclude. We are asking them to feel lost and vulnerable. It is their connection with themselves and with us (see Chapter 6) that sustain them through this in-between.

Curiosity, Play, and Creativity

The unknown is not all grimness and fear; it is creativity's playground. Learning how to not-know is a process. We move from avoiding, to risking vulnerability, through courage, until we arrive at the rewards: curiosity and awe. The shock that freezes us in place for a second when we don't know an answer is a threshold, not a slammed door. It is the orienting response described by Hope and Sugarman (2015). Mild startle creates seconds of poised, alert stillness, in which the pupils dilate and accustomed neural connections uncouple. This is a readiness for re-circuitry, a portal into brain plasticity. "What is this?" is a moment of opportunity. When a patient does not have a preset idea of what will happen next, he is in a position to experience something new.

When we peer into the Grand Canyon for the first time, we are exhilarated, even though our consciousness has never seen anything like it before. The rush of enormity awes us. This is the openness and delight of the mindset of play. We do not have to construct it; it is ours to access naturally.

Play thrives on the absence of predetermined knowns. "In play all definitions slither, dance, combine, break apart, and recombine" says violinist Stephen Nachmanovitch (1990, p. 43). The Cambridge architect, Simon Nicholson echoes Nachmanovitch's observation when he describes playgrounds ideal for promoting children's discovery: "In any environment, both the degree of inventiveness and creativity, and the possibility of discovery, are directly proportional to the number and kind of variables in it" (Nicholson, 1971, as cited in Louv, 2005, p. 86). This was Nicholson's "loose-parts" theory. Incorporating "loose-parts" into the playground of psychotherapy means loosening restraints on what is considered worth talking about and which techniques might help us explore. It means letting go of categories given to us by our theories and allowing the patient and ourselves to mess about naturally with observations that appear as we brainstorm together. This removes pressure for "right" answers. "Playfulness lets us withstand enormous uncertainty," wrote Sarah Lewis (2014, p. 151). This is because play assumes the unknown is a good thing. New discoveries, new connections, new understandings, and new interpretations bloom in such an atmosphere.

We want to encourage play in psychotherapy. A curious, "I don't know," is a lovely way for us to invite mutual exploration. "That's an intriguing idea," "Let's see what emerges next," "What do you think?" are others as well. Even a simple, "I don't know, let's play with that and see where it goes," does wonders for tilting the tone toward exploration and away from fear. It all begins with our own being comfortable as therapists with not-knowing, and our confidence that whatever needs knowing will emerge naturally from noticing, puzzling, connecting, and talking with our patient over time.

I asked Cathy, "I see a look moving across your face. What are you noticing as you hear yourself saying what you just told me?"

Cathy gave a startle and sat up straight, not because a light bulb of discovery had gone off but because my question had put her on alert. Her mind came to attention, arming itself with pre-learned knowledge. "That I'm projecting feelings onto you that I actually feel toward my mother?" She responded as if being called upon in class.

"Is that an idea you looked for in your head or is it a feeling, a realization bubbling up on its own inside inside you?" I asked.

Cathy looked sheepish. "It's in my head."

"It's ok. This isn't a test. I really didn't have any idea in my own head of what you meant by what you first said. I was just curious what it felt like for you as you listened to yourself saying it. What kinds of sensations you had, what pictures floated up. They don't have to make sense. Let's just see what shows up."

Playful thinking allows for seemingly unrelated ideas to be true at the same time. It loves diversity. Silly asides, sober reflections, hunches, thought fragments, rough drafts, and elegant syntheses are all welcome. One truth doesn't erase another. I can be excited *and* scared. When her community was quarantined during the Covid-19 virus, Ellen felt "safe" ("We're being well taken care of") *and* "fatalistic" ("There's nothing much we can do; what's going to happen is going to happen"). We may not know how two, three, or four contradictory truths "fit" together into the mental frameworks we already have, but our need for them to "fit" may reflect a limitation of our human brain, not a quality of reality. We may need to design new frameworks! Or a system without frames or boxes at all. I am fond of saying, "Let's brainstorm together," "What is your personal theory about that?" or "We don't know how it fits together, *yet*." Playful thinking is complex, and it begins quite simply.

Playful thinking creates hypotheses, not conclusions. We encourage our patient to lay the bits of what she's seen, felt, and realized on an imaginary table floating in front of the two of us and consider multiple ways in which they can be arranged into new combinations of meaning. We suspend critical judgment and embrace the adventure of "what if this" or "maybe that." It is not an intellectual exercise. It is sensory, much like trying on clothes and feeling into how they make us appear or sensing the rhythm of a musical beat.

Playful thinking wonders rather than knows. It understands that mistakes are our teachers. As an art teacher once told my daughter, "There are no mistakes in art, just opportunities for new directions." When my patient tells me of a mishap despite her best intentions, I might say, "That's helpful. We can learn from that. It helps us figure out the ingredients that work and the ones that don't." It is equally reassuring to remind our patients that, "Nothing is set in stone." Psychotherapy in its best spirit of exploration is like Christopher Robin and Winnie the Pooh poking around together in puddles on a rainy day, experimenting with making leaf boats and twig masts. Therapy is discovery.

Playful thinking turns endpoints into beginnings. When Ellen says with finality, "I got angry and yelled. That's what I do. I don't stop and think, I just yell," I pause and consider. "Are you saying that's it, that's who you are and there's no changing it?"

Ellen startles with awareness. "No, that's not it. I *want* to be different."

"So what happened next? After you yelled?"

Ellen stared and thought. "I got him the form he wanted. I sat down and helped. We figured it out."

"That's interesting," I said. "So you yelled *and* you helped. Both. You got angry *and* you put your thinking cap on."

"I felt sorry for him and bad about yelling."

"Ok. Those too then. You yelled. And you helped, problem-solved, felt regret, and felt compassion. Hmmm. Maybe the anger and the yelling's a signal for something. Let's figure that out. It's helpful that you noticed it and described it so clearly just now."

Playful thinking is finding the interesting questions inside declarations and putting semicolons where the patient has pasted on a period. "What happened next," is a way out of a seeming dead end.

Playful thinking is pleasurable. It is interest, joy, and delight. Not-knowing, once we lose our fear of it, is liberating, a blank slate of possibilities. It is a momentary mind purge that allows room for new thinking. As Bryan Magee (2016) put it, "The only honest way to live and think is in the fullest possible acknowledgment of our ignorance" (p. 124).

Practicing

We come once again to the critical element of practicing. As we discussed in Chapter 1, all growth requires repetition to root and take hold. This is no different for the ability to not-know.

We therapists are the linchpin to our patients' practicing this skill. The more comfortable we are with not having answers or next steps right away, the more opportunities we will afford our patients to resist concluding, endure not-knowing, identify discomforts about uncertainty, and master uneasiness to the point of being able to feel the rewards that being able to not-know brings.

When as therapists we speak up too hastily to offer a solution or name the reason why our patient thought or did something, it betrays *our* unease, even if we are unaware of being uneasy. Sometimes therapists feel an acute sensation of not "doing" anything or not "doing" enough when they are not talking. They don't realize the doing that is involved in witnessing and being with the patient. Witnessing with steadiness is a powerfully organizing and stabilizing force. Atticus Finch in *To Kill a Mockingbird* (Lee, 1960) was not a loquacious man, yet he commanded respect and effected calm by allowing words to settle and claim their real estate in a room. We can do the same. We can wait patiently with our patient, taking her in, allowing her to find her own thoughts rather than distracting her prematurely with ours. This models what staying present looks like when one doesn't know what another person is going to say or where the conversation might lead. We may feel restless, uneasy, or confusedly brain fogged. None of these sensations need panic us. We can notice them with curiosity and without judgment. Our sensations are always windows into information that is embedded in our patient's telling. When we don't know why we're having the responses we are having, we can voice this: "I find myself having difficulty tracking the thread of your story. I can feel your wanting to tell me something important, but I can't tell just what that is. What are *you* feeling right now, as you tell it to me?" If our uneasiness stems from our patient's looking to us for guidance that isn't yet clear enough to us to give, we can share that fact: "I'm not sure what to do either. But I know if we sit here long enough and keep sharing our thoughts, what to do will emerge naturally. It always does for us." Such interchanges give our patient a concrete, sensory feel for what not running from not-knowing looks like. This is part of practicing.

When we have moments in which we feel shaky about whether not-knowing is a trustworthy method, we can return to Bion (1967/2013), whose wisdom began this chapter. He was confident, "Out of the darkness and formlessness something evolves" (p. 136).

We move next to the essence that holds everything together in psychotherapy: relationship.

References

Bion, W. (2013). Notes on memory and desire. In J. Aguayo & B. Malin (Eds.), *Wilfred Bion: Los Angeles seminars and supervision*. London, UK: Karnac. (Original work published 1967)

Eastwood, C. (Director). (2014). *American sniper* [Film]. Warner Bros. Pictures.

Frenkel-Brunswik, E. (1949). Intolerance of ambiguity as an emotional and perceptual personality variable. *Journal of Personality, 18*(1), 108–143.

Gladwell, M. (2005). *Blink*. New York, NY: Little, Brown and Company.

Gladwell, M. (2008). *Outliers: The story of success*. New York, NY: Little, Brown and Company.

Groopman, J. (2007). *How doctors think*. New York, NY: Houghton Mifflin Company.

Gut, E. (1982). Cause and function of the depressed response: A hypothesis. *International Review of Psycho-Analysis, 9*(2), 179–189.

Harlem, A. (2010). Exile as a dissociative state: When a Self is "lost in transit." *Psychoanalytic Psychology, 27*(4), 460–474.

Hope, A.E., & Sugarman, L.I. (2015). Orienting hypnosis. *American Journal of Clinical Hypnosis, 57*(3), 212–229.

Kahneman, D. (2011). *Thinking, fast and slow*. New York, NY: Farrar, Straus and Giroux.

King, L.A., & Hicks, J.A. (2007). Whatever happened to "What might have been"? Regrets, happiness, and maturity. *American Psychologist, 62*(7), 625–636.

Lee, H. (1960). *To kill a mockingbird*. Philadelphia, PA: J. B. Lippincott & Co.

Lewis, S. (2014). *The rise: Creativity, the gift of failure, and the search for mastery*. New York, NY: Simon & Schuster.

Louv, R. (2005). *Last child in the woods: Saving our children from nature-deficit disorder*. Chapel Hill, NC: Algonquin Books of Chapel Hill.

Lowry, L. (1993). *The giver*. New York, NY: Bantam Doubleday Dell Publishing Group, Inc.

Magee, B. (2016). *Ultimate questions*. Princeton, NJ: Princeton University Press.

Mayer, E.L. (2007). *Extraordinary knowing: Science, skepticism, and the inexplicable powers of the human mind*. New York, NY: Bantam Books.

McGilchrist, I. (2009). *The master and his emissary*. New Haven, CT: Yale University Press.

Nachmanovitch, S. (1990). *Free play: Improvisation in life and art*. New York, NY: Penguin Putnam, Inc.

Rosenthal, R. (1966). *Experimenter effects in behavioral research*. New York, NY: Appleton-Century-Crofts.

Rosenthal, R. (1976). *Experimenter effects in behavioral research: Enlarged edition*. New York, NY: Irvington Publishers.

Rosenthal, R., & Jacobson, L. (1968). *Pygmalion in the classroom: Teacher expectations and pupils' intellectual development.* New York, NY: Holt, Rinehart & Winston.

Rovelli, C. (2017). *Reality is not what it seems* (S. Carnell & E. Segre, trans.). New York, NY: Riverhead Books.

Zetzel, E.R. (1965). Depression and the incapacity to bear it. In M. Schur (Ed.), *Essays in memory of Marie Bonaparte* (pp. 243–274). New York, NY: International Universities Press.

6 Relationship

When I have been listened to and when I have been heard, I am able to reperceive my world in a new way and to go on. It is astonishing how elements that seem insoluble become soluble when someone listens.
—Carl Rogers, *A Way of Being*

The ability of therapists to establish and maintain a good alliance has been greatly overestimated ... Human beings have enormous difficulty dealing with interpersonal conflict in which they are participants. (Binder & Strupp, 1997, p. 121)

The most troubling and difficult to manage places of feeling stuck in psychotherapy are the ones inside the connection between ourselves and our patient.

A "positive therapeutic alliance" is the strongest predictor there is of good psychotherapy outcome. However, what is not explained often enough is how difficult it is to provide that positive alliance. "Negative therapeutic process" pervades the work between patient and therapist and is difficult to manage. When not managed well, it leads to poor psychotherapy outcome and can even cause harm.

Let us look first at how we need to be as therapists, then at what mars our efforts, and finally we'll consider what we can do to be better.

The Potently Positive Force That Is Relationship

When different disciplines with different perspectives, databases, and vocabulary arrive at the same conclusions time after time, we have found a kernel of truth. One of these truths is: positive relationship is at the core of human growth and healing.

Consider the evidence: infants who are not sufficiently cuddled fail to grow. Their physical health deteriorates; sometimes they die. Food is not enough; being held by human hands is a critical nutrient (Crandall, 1897; Spitz, 1945). It is the same for adults. Adults with fewer relationships

DOI: 10.4324/9781315449043-6

deteriorate physically. They develop more illnesses. They die sooner. It seems as if networks of relationships keep the human spirit alive (Berkman & Syme, 1979; DiJulio et al., 2018; Holt-Lunstad et al., 2015; Holt-Lunstad et al., 2010; Housman & Dorman, 2005; Umberson & Montez, 2010; Wright, 2016).

It's not just our bodies that are nurtured and energized by relationships; our minds are too. Infants, school-age children, and adults learn more information and retain it better when they learn *in relationship* with people (Conboy et al., 2015; Dikker et al., 2017; Kuhl et al., 2003; Lytle et al., 2018; Piazza et al., 2020; Wass et al., 2018). This is such a powerful effect that we see it even with nine-month-old infants crawling near a floor-mounted, eye-level (for the infants), 24-inch television screen (Lytle et al., 2018) displaying a video of a Chinese-speaking adult. The infants from monolingual English-speaking households retain more Mandarin Chinese sounds after crawling on the floor *if* they have been crawling near the television screen *with* a newly met nine-month-old infant rather than by themselves!

Given the impact that relationship has on growing the body and mind it is not surprising to learn that it has a critical impact on *healing* the body and mind. Even placebos work better when they are administered within a positive relationship (Benedetti, 2011, 2013, 2014a, 2014b; Derra & Schwab, 2013; Evers et al., 2018; Nakano et al., 1998). The more meaningful the doctor-patient relationship the more likely patients are to take their psychiatric medications (Ehret & Wang, 2013; Julius et al., 2009; Velligan et al., 2009). Pain and stress are reduced when one is touched by a human hand, whether you are an infant hooked up with tubes in the NICU or an adult undergoing a procedure or stressful moment (Fatollahzade et al., 2020; Geri et al., 2019; Graff et al., 2019; Herrington & Chiodo, 2014). When the anesthesiologist simply pays surgical patients a brief visit before an operation, says hello, and forms rapport, the visit calms patients more effectively than a sedative injection and they ask for less pain medication after surgery (Benson, 1997; Egbert & Jackson, 2013). And in psychotherapy? The quality of the relationship between psychotherapist and patient predicts positive outcome more robustly than any other factor. This has held true across decades of research, looking at intensive therapy and brief therapy; naturalistic settings and controlled settings; psychodynamic, cognitive, cognitive-behavioral therapy and interpersonal, experiential, and eclectic therapy; from substance abuse to major depression to interpersonal problems; assessed by patients, therapists, and independent observers; and working with Psychologists, Psychiatrists, and Social Workers (Ardito & Rabellino, 2011; Binder & Strupp, 1997; Gardner et al., 2020; Geller & Porges, 2014; Lipner et al., 2019; Peebles, 2012, pp. 43–55).

More interested in the reverse focus of avoiding negative reprisals if your interventions don't work? Then know that the risk of malpractice suits following unhappy medical outcomes is lower when there has been a positive connection between doctor and patient (Miglioretti et al., 2018; Moore et al., 2000; Trumble et al., 2006; Virshup et al., 1999).

These studies are just a small sample of the available research. The full scope of evidence fills volumes.

Igniting Relationship's Positive Energy in Psychotherapy: A "Therapeutic Alliance"

Interestingly, the therapeutic alliance that leads to good outcomes is not about establishing a friendship or making sure our patient feels good. It is not about reassurance, flattery, or being careful not to disagree. To ignite relationship's positive energy in psychotherapy so that the relationship becomes an alliance that unlocks change requires empathy, warmth, authenticity, shared goals, and the synchronization of rhythms of attention and inattention, activation and calming.

To understand a little about empathy, warmth, and authenticity, let's go back to the theologian/philosopher Martin Buber (1923/1970). Buber grasped the mystery of how humans make each other feel they matter; it happens when we stay fully present with another person while they are expressing themselves and do so without judgment or ulterior motives. Witnessing another person unconditionally is an exchange of energy that Buber called an "encounter." This encounter is powerful; it allows the other person to feel himself taking up space and becoming tangible as he experiences himself materializing in the listener's mind. He feels phenomenologically that he has physical substance or matter rather than subjectively feeling as if he is ethereal or invisible to others. This enlarges the expression, "I matter," deepening it to include a sensory as well as emotional experience. Something more is taking place than just feeling heard. When we listen and stay-with another in the way Buber intended we are bringing another person's self into being. This power to create in each other a sensation of being real is so deeply essential as to be sacred.

Carl Rogers (1961, 1980) understood the powerful actualization taking place inside Buber's encounter. He broke down three ingredients that Buber's kind of listening held: empathy, warmth, and genuineness or authenticity as a person. Each of these three traits acts as a check and balance on the other. For example, warmth *with* empathy centers us in our patient's experience and avoids our offering as faux warmth a lively chatter about ourselves or the solicitation of details that interest us. Authenticity tames charisma, which sometimes tries to pass for warmth, and tempers it with the vulnerability of being our unvarnished selves, humbly witnessing instead of trying to dazzle. The chemistry of empathy, warmth, and authenticity creates a relational environment of trust and respect, in which the personhood and autonomy of the patient are tantamount.

Bordin (1979) added a critical twist to this trio, one that tightened therapeutic relationship into therapeutic alliance. His twist was "shared focus." A shared focus with shared goals turns therapist and patient into working partners who are working *together* toward goals that are *mutually* agreed upon (Ardito & Rabellino, 2011).

Finally, the combined work of Winnicott (1953), Brazelton, Tronick, Porges, and Schore added a finishing touch which addressed the dynamism of therapeutic alliance. This is the energy flow of synchronicity of rhythms. *We are wired to feel the rhythms of other humans.* Infants as young as two-three weeks respond to inanimate objects differently than they do to people. With objects, they swipe and bat in jerky movements, "knowing" them with their hands. In contrast, with people, infants' eyes and bodies tune into rhythmic interactions, "knowing" a person through mutual, synchronized, energy cycles of attention and inattention, activation and calming (Brazelton et al., 1975). In fact, a mother "grows" her infant through this synchronization. When a mother syncs up with her infant, attuning to his energy level when he engages and quieting and waiting for him when he turns away, her syncing regulates the physical rhythms of her baby's organs, heart, breathing, sleeping, and eating (Brazelton et al., 1975). It expands her baby's consciousness, gradually enlarging his way of knowing the world. As Mary Oliver (2016) reflects, "The child whose gaze is met learns that the world is real, and desirable—that the child himself is real, and cherished" (p. 83). Adult human relationships are similar. People take in each other *through the body not just the mind* in wave-rhythms, waves of electrical impulses in the brain, respiration, heart-rate, blood pressure, muscle tension/coordination, and vocal pitch. They continuously send, receive, and respond through these energy signals bidirectionally with or without words. In psychotherapy, patients and therapists synchronize their rhythms of breathing, heart rate, motor tension, and motor movements as their mutual involvement in the psychotherapy process deepens (Banyai et al., 1982; Linton et al., 1977). This is the "right brain to right brain" communication of which Daniel Schore (1994, 2009) speaks. What turns right brain to right brain communication in psychotherapy into a therapeutic alliance is the therapist's ability to be aware of and regulate his own emotional activation and parasympathetic tone (Ham & Tronick, 2009), while sensitively resonating with and leading his patient's energy and consciousness. This delicate dance of synchronizing attention and inattention, activation and calming, "grows" his and his patient's fields of consciousness (Tronick, 2001, 2007) and modulates their autonomic nervous systems (Geller & Porges, 2014) completing the picture of what activates positive energy in a therapeutic relationship.

Relationships Carry Negative Potential As Well

If we turn the energy of relationship over, we find a darker side: the power to devastate, not grow.

Physical neglect is obviously unhealthy; children and adults need food, shelter, and clothing to survive. The damage caused by emotional neglect on the other hand is insidious; it silently withers the human spirit. Neglect *fails* to acknowledge; it fails to hold in mind. The person feels himself *not*-existing in others' minds and eventually begins feeling he does not exist at all. He feels invisible. This is more than a metaphor; it is a palpable physicality; it is the literal *absence of activation* of the other's neural and sensory sparks engaging with and answering one's own energy signals. We require the sensory feedback, the vitalization caused by our signals pinging and quickening energy in another in order to feel real. Absence of that mutual sparking of human electricity snuffs the growth of a person's life force the same way absence of oxygen snuffs fire. This is why emotionally neglected humans may describe themselves feeling alien or as if they are drifting in a dark void, like space. Sometimes emotional neglect's erasure is sharper, such as Amish shunning or social media's "ghosting," which eradicate with intention; i.e., "You no longer exist." More often, however, neglect works its harm quietly, with no drama: not-hearing, overlooking, not-remembering, ignoring, withdrawing, being impassive, or watching vacantly.

The neglected babies Rene Spitz (1945) observed in orphanages were not held, and the light went out in their eyes. They failed to grow and some died. The babies Edward Tronick (UMass Boston, 2009) observed were physically and emotionally healthy to start with. They'd had months of good-enough mothering with predictable-enough synchronization back and forth but still they were undone by just a few minutes of simulated emotional neglect. Tronick's experimental design, called the "Still-Face" experiment, captured on video infants' delight as they engaged with their mothers' bright cooing and also captured their dramatic shift when mother followed instructions to offer no emotional response, no facial expression, and no vocalization. When mother became unresponsive, her baby tried desperately to engage her, became confused and agitated when nothing he did succeeded, and from there rapidly deteriorated into having trouble organizing emotions and body. His arms flailed, his legs kicked jerkily, he arched his back, and emitted squawky cries.

The effects of prolonged withdrawal of physical and emotional engagement carry into adulthood. Vincent Felitti, a psychiatrist with Kaiser Permanente working with obese patients in a weight loss program, stumbled onto a discovery through a misstated screening question that uncovered the fact that a disproportionate number of his obese patients had suffered childhood trauma. This led to 30 years of follow-up investigations following over 17,000 patients, some for 15 years, in conjunction with the Centers for Disease Control (CDC). Named the Adverse Childhood Experiences (ACE) studies, these investigations found that people who checked two or more items on a ten-item scale of negative childhood events suffered higher rates of problems which included ischemic heart disease, stroke, chronic bronchitis or emphysema, diabetes, hepatitis, chronic obstructive pulmonary disease (COPD), chronic depression, alcoholism, absenteeism from work, serious financial problems, and serious problems with job performance than did those who said they'd experienced 0 or 1 event (Adverse Childhood Experiences, n.d.; Felitti et al., 1998). The incidence of problems rose in direct proportion to the number of items checked. Two of the ten ACE items tap neglect: "Often felt that no one in your family loved you or thought you were important or special, or felt your family didn't look out for each other, feel close to each other, or support each other." "Often felt you didn't have enough to eat, had to wear dirty clothes, and had no one to protect you" (Schulman & Maul, 2019).

Neglect's power is universally understood. One of the strongest curses in the Hebrew language is the phrase, yimakh shemo ("May his name be erased"). Another Jewish saying echoes this power of humans to evaporate each other: "You die twice. The first time when your body dies; the second when your name is spoken for the last time."

Hostility is the second weapon of the dark side of relationship. It actively inflicts pain without necessarily aiming to eliminate the person. Obvious examples are physical attacks or torture; their destruction is indisputable. Implicit hostility leaves scars as well. Verbal humiliation, belittling, blaming, contempt, and subjugating cause damage. Young adults commit suicide or commit violence in the wake of being shamed and bullied online or in classroom. The ACE questionnaire includes questions about hostility. "A parent or other adult in the household often swore at you, insulted you, put you down, or humiliated you, or acted in a way that made you afraid that you might be physically hurt." "A parent or other adult in the household often pushed, grabbed, or threw something at you, or ever hit you so hard that you had marks or were injured" (Schulman & Maul, 2019).

When non-physical hostility combines with gaslighting or double-bind communication (Bateson et al., 1956), it not only damages, it makes the other person feel crazy and doubt themselves as well. In Sartre's chilling play about Hell, *No Exit* (1945/1958), he unmasks the misuse of empathy. The playwright throws three people into a locked room and watches them slowly shred each other's souls. Sartre understands the importance of being "seen," and throughout shifting schemes of exploitation and deception, each character at some point is invited into being explicitly taken in by the other's eyes. Once they acquiesce, they are hostilely distorted, "devoured .... bogged ... stolen" by eyes that accuse and take over parasitically rather than seeing compassionately and accurately. "When I can't see myself I begin to wonder if I really and truly exist," murmurs Estelle anxiously (p. 11).

"Negative Therapeutic Process"

Perhaps you wonder why the deep dive into neglect and hostility. We went there because these are the two elements found in negative therapeutic process.

Hans Strupp began researching therapy's relational process in the 1950s. He examined different theoretical approaches. As technology advanced his methods of observation advanced and his data analyses kept pace with sophisticated statistics. His group's studies were not questionnaire-dependent. They used videotapes of therapy sessions; transcripts rated by independent raters; interviews of patients and therapists; and in some cases, interviews with supervisors. Strupp and colleagues amassed a body of work that was one of the most significant contributions to psychotherapy outcome research that we have, so it's no small matter when at the age of 76, Strupp reviewed his prodigious collection of findings with his colleague Jefferey Binder and concluded that, "negative therapeutic process is pervasive, enormously destructive to the therapeutic relationship, and extremely difficult for therapists to manage" (Binder & Strupp, 1997, p. 134).

We have known since we began keeping track in the 1950s that about one-third of patients drop out of psychotherapy (Peebles, 2018). We know too that therapists can do harm to patients; about 7–8% of patients are worse by the end of treatment (Bergin, 1966; Hannan et al., 2005; Lambert et al., 2002; Peebles, 2018). Strupp's work pins down specifics: negative feelings in psychotherapy are ubiquitous; patients tend to hide their negative feelings from their therapists; therapists tend to hide their negative feelings from themselves; negative feelings tend to go undetected and unaddressed; and the outcome of therapy is in the balance (Binder & Strupp, 1997; Hannan et al., 2005). This all happens inside micro-exchanges. Small interplays or quips, carrying explicit or implicit messages of attacking, belittling, or blaming (i.e., hostility), or ignoring, rejecting, appeasing, or walling off (i.e., neglect), hurt and provoke. When therapist or patient gets hooked by the provocation and responds in kind, damage accumulates. One or both parties disengages. If this glitched process is not identified at some point and talked about constructively, there is termination of the relationship and dissatisfaction.

It is not only Strupp's group that has identified this dynamic. Multiple groups working from different angles report the same findings. The marital therapist, John Gottman (1994), documented moment-to-moment, time-series analyses of exchanges between hundreds of spousal pairs. Messages of criticism, contempt, defensiveness, and stonewalling predict early divorce. In other words, attack (hostility) and withdrawal (neglect).

Jeremy Safran, Christopher Muran, and dozens of their colleagues in the New York City area have worked on nuances of the therapeutic alliance since the late 1980s. They too found negative feelings between therapist and patient to be not only "common" but "inevitable" (Gardner et al., 2020, p. 176). The Safran-Muran network of researchers dubbed these breaches, "ruptures," and identified two types. There are withdrawal ruptures signaled by a patient's sudden silence, avoiding answering a question, minimal responses, sudden topic shifts, hiding negative feelings, or making nice and trying to smooth things over with the therapist. There are confrontation ruptures involving a patient's open expression of anger or dissatisfaction with the therapist or the therapy, disagreement with goals, defensiveness, or trying to control or pressure the therapist.

Clinician-Researchers working from a psychophysiological orientation called Polyvagal Theory also reach similar conclusions organized under a different rubric, that of the autonomic nervous system's detection and response system for safety and threat (Geller & Porges, 2014). Threat is perceived when a person attacks or withdraws; i.e., hostility and neglect. Detecting threat triggers self-protections, which activate either our sympathetic nervous system's fight/flight response or activating the less familiar parasympathetic nervous system's freeze response. The latter involves shutting down, closing off, dissociating, and/or disconnecting with feelings and sensations. In psychotherapy, mutual detection systems in therapist and patient continuously interplay. It is not that the therapist or the patient "cause" the problem. The problem becomes an energy field between them of perceived threat. Perhaps the patient detects threat from the therapist—the therapist subtly pulls away, slightly withdraws warmth, or adds a hostile edge to his choice of words—and instantaneously switches on a neural, self-protective fight/flight or freeze response. The therapist senses his patient's tensing or withdrawing and counter-protects with tension or withdrawal himself. As these mutual adjustments to each other continue, at some point the therapist becomes aware of feeling uncomfortable, but usually after the subtle dance of hostility and neglect is already underway.

Psychodynamic clinicians have written about negative feelings in therapy as well, at first primarily about patients' anger. But Winnicott (1949) galvanized a conversation around *therapists'* anger when he wrote, "Hate in the Counter-transference." Since that publication, 600 articles (as of August, 2020) touching on "hate" with "countertransference" are listed in the database of PepWeb (Psychoanalytic Electronic Publishing). Many, such as Glen Gabbard's (1991), offer snippets of transcripts and personal revelations permitting us a raw peek into the pain that a tangled and prolonged rupture brings.

Being inside a negative therapeutic process is not a dispassionate experience. And how could it be? If, as we understand from the beginning of this chapter, social relationships form the essence of nourishment for our life force as humans, then safety and threat inside relationship are of utmost importance, matters of emotional life and death. When feeling stuck in therapy is more than an intellectual puzzle around technical error and instead gets under our skin, it takes refined training, well developed emotional resources, and a heavy dose of humility to be able to feel what we're feeling and use those feelings as information to recognize and untangle ourselves and our patient from a highly personal, interpersonal mess. "In our study [of highly experienced, professional therapists] we failed to encounter a single instance in which a difficult patient's hostility and negativism were successfully confronted or resolved ... therapists' negative responses to difficult patients are far more common and far more intractable than has been generally recognized," wrote Strupp (1980, p. 954).

The intractability of negative therapeutic process is no longer as dire as Strupp witnessed 40 years ago. Research has spurred attention to this problem and tools have developed. There is consensus that the key to becoming unstuck, when something in the relationship itself is the problem, is being able to: (1) detect negative feelings when they emerge in us or in our patient; (2) slow down our own hurt, anger, confusion, or defensiveness; curb anxious impulses to deny, defend, explain, or otherwise "fix" the feelings; and instead listen and reflect until we have a better grasp of the matter; and (3) talk with our patient about the negative energy with the calm and respect that comes from knowing how to learn from negative process rather than be railroaded by it. These three guidelines are not easy to accomplish; to do so requires training, practice, and personal therapy. However, if you want to help patients grow, it is worth the investment. A therapist's ability to recognize and work constructively with ruptures is significantly tied to patients' improvement in therapy (Gardner et al., 2020); it not only saves a positive therapeutic alliance, it strengthens it.

Unspoken Communication

I want to briefly recall something I mentioned in Chapter 4: our intent and our interior feelings are transmitted to our patients even if we don't speak them. This happens especially when we try to hide feelings from ourselves. Only psychopaths can effortlessly fool people.

How does this transmission of unspoken inner feelings work? Is it our "mirror neurons," brain cells deep in our frontal lobes that seem wired to "reenact in our own brains what other people do" (Iacoboni, 2008, p. 200)? Is it our patient "projecting" feelings into us and our "identifying" with the feelings they project, the "projective identification" of which psychoanalysts write (Horwitz, 1983)? Is it the "right brain to right brain" communication that Allan Schore (1994, 2009), building on Brazelton (Brazelton et al., 1975) and Tronick (Tronick, 2007; Tronick et al., 1978), explains is so vital to infant development and therapeutic listening? Is it "entrainment," the natural synchronization of waveforms in mechanical and biological systems in close enough proximity, caused by the mutually exerted tugs of energy that eventually align the oscillations of energy?

As when clock pendulums synchronize their swinging, washing machines synchronize their spinning, and therapists and patients in good alliance synchronize their breathing, heart rate, and muscle tension (see Peebles, 2018, pp. 249–250)? Is it the neuroanatomically based, "face-to-heart" vagal circuitry connecting facial expressions, verbal prosody, and their detection in others with parasympathetic and sympathetic nervous system activations and calming (Geller & Porges, 2014)? Is it a form of "extraordinary knowing" or telepathy? There is documentation of therapists anticipating a patient's associations before they are spoken or patients dreaming of events in a therapist's life for which they could have had no knowledge (Lazar, 2001; Mayer, 2001, 2007). There is probably something of each of these concepts, each of which reaches toward explanation, but none of which fully lays out exactly how unspoken communication occurs.

What we do know something about is the form unspoken communication takes (Moss & Gengerelli, 1967, 1970), and this is worth paying attention to so we understand what we are listening for and what our patient is hearing. Unspoken knowing is not receiving literal transcripts of another's thoughts in sentence form. It arrives in the shape that dreams and poetry take; i.e., in impressions, images, sensations, or sounds like melodies or clang associations. These "pop" or float into mind rather than march forth in orderly fashion when summoned. These impressions are rich condensations of meaning. They *approximate* the experience of another person through associational links rather than reproduce it exactly. It is the grammar used in right-hemispheric processing (McGilchrist, 2009) and what Freud called "primary process thinking," which researchers have found to be a marker of creativity in stable people (Holt, 2002). It contrasts with linear thinking in the same way that colorful, video-maps reshaping across time contrast with flat, black lines drawn in static grid-form against a white background (Tufte, 1983, 2006).

Howard Gardner, a developmental psychologist at Harvard, believed that the ability to read such communications in others and in ourselves was a special kind of intelligence (Gardner, 1983). In synthesizing data from different cultures, experts, empirical findings, and neurobiological findings, Gardner found that IQ could not be boiled down to only verbal and math abilities. There are five other intelligences as well: Musical, Spatial (engineers, architects), Bodily-Kinesthetic (athletes, dancers), Interpersonal (teachers, leaders, healers), and Intra-personal (novelists, therapists).

Because we chose to be therapists, it is likely we were born with sensitivities to emotional nuances and the grammar of unspoken communication in the same way a musician is sensitive to pitch, rhythm, and harmony. But every talent needs training to blossom into expertise. A therapist's training grounds are instruction, supervision, and personal therapy.

Instruction

Several instructional approaches to recognizing and working produc-
tively with negative feelings have passed the test of empirical and clinical
replication. There is Lambert's feedback model, the Safran-Muran
group's rupture repair model, the psychodynamic transference/counter-
transference model, and the Porges mindfulness Presence model. It is
worth learning one of these methods well, and ideally more than one.
They are not incompatible; they complement each other. It is outside the
scope of this book to teach them; I will simply highlight particular ways
each is useful. I list them in order of how much psychological reflection
and daily personal practice each requires, from least to most.

Feedback

The Feedback method gives therapists algorithmic feedback every few sessions about whether or not their patient's experience fits a probability
trajectory for getting better, or heading toward stalling and deteriorating
(Lambert, 2010). With immediate feedback in hand about negative trends,
therapists in 3/4 of cases are able to correct the course of therapy and avert
deterioration by changing clinical strategies, seeking consultation, or
making referrals for adjunctive therapies (Lambert et al., 2002). The
Feedback model has proven particularly useful clinically with patients who
are in greater distress at the start of therapy. The practical value of this
monitoring and feedback has been replicated multiple times, with cognitive-
behavioral, psychodynamic/interpersonal, and humanistic/existential approaches, and with experienced clinicians and trainees. A meta-analysis of
24 such studies recently verified its efficacy (Lambert et al., 2018).

Feedback is calculated from patients' responses to a questionnaire
called the Outcome Questionnaire (OQ-45 or OQ-45.2), which has been
evaluated thus far on tens of thousands of clients. Patients fill it out
before each therapy session; it takes about five to seven minutes to
complete; and asks questions about subjective discomfort, relationships
(loneliness, conflicts with people, marriage and family difficulties), performance of responsibilities in work, school or home, and quality of life
factors. Formulas have been refined for establishing cut-off scores for
four probability cells relative to how seriously distressed the patient was
at the start of therapy and how many sessions they've attended thus far.
These four probability cells are: (1) the patient is feeling good and is
ready to terminate; (2) the patient is making progress toward feeling
better; (3) the patient is changing less than one would expect; and (4) the
patient is at risk for dropping out of therapy prematurely and/or deteriorating. The accuracy of this tool for predicting deterioration is better
than clinical judgment; in one study it accurately identified 100% of the

patients who were at risk for deteriorating by the end of therapy whereas clinicians identified none (Hannan et al., 2005).

Decision-making technology is not meant to replace clinical judgment. It is offered as an assist, like an early-warning system, for therapists to detect problems in the process early enough to give them sufficient time to take preventative action. Empirical studies have established that therapists tend to be too hopeful in the face of worrisome markers; they don't see accurately when feeling stuck requires prompt action. Such a belief in the process is a strength in terms of dedication and optimism, but it becomes a concern when it prevents therapists from changing strategies soon enough to avoid a patient's decline.

Rupture-Repair, Rupture-Resolution

The Safran-Muran group developed a formal training program based on their research findings that teaches clinicians how to recognize and repair ruptures. Being research-based brings advantages: what qualifies as a clinical rupture has been rigorously defined and specific examples of patients' pulling away or feeling dislike are captured on film (e.g., see *therapeutic-alliance.org*). This expedites the process of teaching clinicians what to look for, particularly when it comes to identifying subtler cues such as physical tension, appeasement, veiled insults, and dismissive tones.

This model understands that often it is the *unsettling emotions that ruptures stir in therapists*, such as confusion, incompetence, and guilt, that cause therapists to ignore, miss, or poorly handle tensions. Accordingly, the training emphasizes components that build clinicians' ability to become aware of their feelings and approach their feelings with empathy and curiosity rather than defensiveness, so they can help their patients do the same. Such components include awareness-oriented role plays in which students take turns playing therapist and patient, mindfulness training, and working with a trusted supervisor while viewing video clips of one's own moment-to-moment interactions with patients in order to analyze and learn from these interactions.

Other teaching methods that supplement didactic training include watching videotapes of experienced therapists and learning the research methods of categorizing ruptures.

It is not the presence of ruptures that is a problem; this group's research established—just as Strupp's group did—that negative moments in therapy are common and inevitable. It is when ruptures are not discussed that they impair alliance. Timely detection is critical. When therapists don't recognize strain in the relationship, a patient's symptoms tend to worsen by the next session (Eubanks et al., 2019).

Training in resolving disruptions is not aimed at prescribing scripts because the infinite shadings of upset that can occur between two people cannot be catalogued. Rather the work focuses on developing skills needed for asking about dissatisfaction directly and non-judgmentally, for unpacking sources of upset non-defensively even when the therapist is the source, and for offering understanding, acceptance of responsibility for one's participation, and validation for raising tough issues. These make for a restorative interpersonal experience. When the immediate strain between therapist and patient is repaired, links can be made to similar patterns in the patient's life.

Unfortunately, the kind of ruptures that occur when patients and therapists differ in gender, race, religion, sexual orientation, and socioeconomic status have not yet been systematically researched (Eubanks et al., 2019). Even so, the training model has been systematically researched, and evidence indicates that therapists can get better at recognizing negativity in patients and in themselves and they can learn how to restore the mutuality and reciprocity at the center of relationship's positive, growth-producing energy (Zilcha-Mano et al., 2020). This is promising news.

Transference/Countertransference

Simply (or simplistically) put, transference is the patient's feelings toward the therapist, and countertransference is a therapist's feelings stirred in the relationship with the patient. This is the oldest conceptual rubric used to understand places of feeling stuck inside the therapeutic relationship, and it has undergone multiple refinements across a century of permutations in psychodynamic therapy. The transference-countertransference model underpins the clinical idea of ruptures and repair and informs all approaches that work with relationship as central in psychotherapy. These concepts emerged from clinical observations and qualitative study, not quantitative empirical research, but they earned their bona fides through passing tests of time and clinical relevance (Castonguay et al., 2010). Over 36,000 relevant publications since 1912 are listed in PebWeb's search engine alone as of September 2020. What transference and countertransference may lack in specificity of definition, they make up for in clinical depth, nuance, and insight.

It is the nuggets of practical wisdom from clinicians willing to be transparent about deeper emotional details in their dealings with patients that make this approach irreplaceable. These details have supported the understanding that the energy between patient and therapist forms a field between them, through which interior interpersonal information flows and patterns of response-reaction amplify swiftly. The information transmitted moves both through and outside of awareness, registered even if not consciously "known." To steer through this information so one doesn't harm or gaslight the patient by denying what the patient is picking up but the therapist does not feel comfortable acknowledging, this approach counsels and sometimes requires personal therapy for the therapist. The most beneficial type of personal therapy for doing this type of work is one that allows enough time to learn about one's darker sides, one's inner aspects that only emerge in intimacy, and one's un-worded memories of wounds that play themselves out in sharp-edged comments or obliviousness. Such depth of personal exploration expands what one can hear in a patient's stories; it guards against covertly exploiting the relationship emotionally with the patient to gratify one's needs; and it matures the skill of using one's feelings as a window into a patient's interior world.

To this latter point, Paula Heimann (1950) noticed that what we are feeling as therapists in psychotherapy sessions isn't always, and is never only, about us; instead, our feelings are part of the energy flowing between us and our patient created by close emotional and physical proximity. As such, our feelings may be telling us something about the patient that the patient is unable to describe or even fully know. "The [therapist's] emotional response to his patient ... represents one of the most important tools for his work ... an instrument of research into the patient's unconscious" (p. 82). In Heimann's experience, and in mine, we therapists are like musical instruments. We vibrate with the frequencies that exist in the room with our patient. The skill is in being able to listen, reflect, and inquire in a way that unravels what is us, what is our patient, and what is the chemistry sparked by particular issues in each of us meeting in that moment. It is difficult to teach this skill.

Feeling into places of interpersonal tension rather than pulling away from them can open growth opportunities, for both patient and therapist. For example, in a psychotherapy session with Frida, something flipped in her like a light switch. About three sentences of mine ago, her face had arranged itself into a forbearing smile. She had stopped explaining her boss' bullying behavior; now she seemed to be marshaling energy to endure my commentary and avoid openly criticizing me for obviously missing her point. This made me squirm. What had happened? I thought I'd been helping. I could feel a familiarity in being uncomfortably caught off guard; Frida and I had been here before. I went still and felt my way inward. Once quiet, I sensed twinges of pain inside me, sadness, a bit of shame, and there it was—hopelessness. I felt as if I'd been brought up short, exposed as self-focused, oblivious, and foolish in my insensitivity. Frida communicated a sort of submission to something inevitable and at the same time there was a hint of knowingly exposing me as pompous. It is difficult to describe how I was feeling myself inside the person Frida was experiencing me to be, while simultaneously not experiencing it to be me exactly. Frida was waiting for the clock to run out on our session and looking forward to being alone as a reprieve from being with me. As these sensory-filled revelations became clear to me, I ventured a tentative description of them to Frida. Her eyes grew wide; she quickly composed her face.

"Yes," she said, "I *am* enduring. I want the session to be over. This is useless and I don't know what else to do."

I wanted to bridge our two realities. I paused, mentally stumbling because I didn't want Frida to feel I was papering my reality over hers. I spoke slowly, feeling my way along the outlines of my sensations. "The useless feeling is coming through," I said. "You're helping me feel it *from the inside*. I can *see* you enduring right now, how you're trying not to feel pain and how the only thing left is to tell yourself that it will soon be over. You're trying to hide from me your feeling that I'm failing you, yet you're showing it to me too. Nothing feels good. Nothing feels possible, and inside this place anything you could think to say *is* useless. But all this you're *communicating* to me. I'm feeling it. You're not alone in it like you were growing up. I see you feeling it. It feels useless, and I'm feeling that useless feeling with you."

At that moment Frida felt understood, despite having felt I was not understanding. She experienced being heard even while she felt anything she said was useless. These paradoxes forced her mind to reorganize. Her field of consciousness about what was inevitable between two people expanded to include a new possibility.

This is what growth looks like: tiny steps of expanding awareness. My personal reflections had held more information than I'd spoken aloud to Frida; I was selective in what I said to her because one understanding at a time is the only way a mind can absorb new ways of thinking.

Heinrich Racker (1957) expanded Heimann's ideas. He loosely organized the reverberations we feel in our patient's presence into three spaces. Sometimes our feelings sample what the patient is feeling, as when I felt the sad, hopeless feelings that Frida was feeling. Sometimes our feelings sample how other people have responded toward our patient in his past, as in the case of my feeling as if I'd been oblivious and insensitive with Frida. Sometimes our feelings are reactions ignited by the way our patient is acting that touches a nerve of how we were treated and people we lived with in our past, as in the shame I felt when I felt I had been caught talking too much about myself. These different streams of information twirl through us. Too often we become horrified if we discover anything less than compassion in ourselves. We don't know how to let ourselves linger long enough in feared emotions to discover the gold of information in them. Racker (1957) saw a therapist's "continuity and depth of his conscious contact with himself" (p. 308) to be vital to mining this gold, just as Eubanks et al. (2019) saw the therapist's "ability to attend to the here and now with an attitude of curiosity and nonjudgmental acceptance" (p. 573) to be vital to becoming unstuck.

Harold Searles (1979), a psychoanalyst with an uncanny ability to hear what was not being said, believed that stuck places in psychotherapy stem inevitably from places the therapist is having trouble figuring out in his own life. We can only take a patient as far as we have gone ourselves. Searles' twist of understanding was that a patient's being stuck was an indirect attempt to heal the therapist by forcing the therapist to confront and fix something inside himself that blocks his ability to help the patient move forward. This is especially true for patients who stay in therapy despite feeling stuck; they want us to succeed in helping them and somehow they believe we can. Theodor Reik (1948), coiner of the phrase, "listening with the third ear," wrote, "In almost all of them [places of feeling stuck in the therapy relationship] there was also a hindrance in myself that blocked me or dulled the sharpness of my observation (p. 155)." The transference/countertransference model focuses therapists on the foibles they bring to their attempts to heal others and encourages them to sort through their histories to better serve their patients. This is time-tested advice; e.g., "Physician, heal thyself" (Luke 4:23, King James Version).

Therapeutic Presence

Mental health does not depend only on what we think or feel. One's physical self is also a key component. Therapy is fuller when therapists know how to help a patient listen to the information from his body and when they understand how to settle their own bodies so they can help their patient soothe his. Mindfulness and therapeutic presence are ways of doing both.

Traditional psychotherapy left the body behind. This is a problem. As we discussed in Chapter 4, intentionally registering and rehearsing new experiences in a sensory bodily way is necessary for fully embodying new experiences of self, others, and the world. We cause our patient to lose contact with himself if we talk only with his mind and its ideas without hearing from his body with its heart rate and breathing, or talk only to his brain and its neurochemicals without giving audience to the wounds and memories in his heart, or encourage only the logical precision of his intellect without helping him validate equally the truths of emotional knowledge from his gut and soul. Dividing a person into brain, mind, body, heart, or soul does not bring solutions that feel complete because a human being is no one of those things. He is the symphony of all of them.

Mindfulness derives in part from the Buddhist tradition of decreasing suffering by learning how to draw one's mind away from regrets about the past and fears about the future into the present moment instead. It also echoes the Taoist message of contentment resting inside simplicity of experiencing what is there instead of rushing to categorize knowledge and proclaim conclusions when there is so much that we cannot know. People like Thich Nhat Hanh (1975) and Benjamin Hoff (1982) made such thinking accessible to western minds by writing in light, lucid prose that did not chide the reader for living inside modernity and technology and did not require one to retreat from the world in order to feel calm. Rather, it offered a steadying way of withstanding the roiling of the world through quieting one's physical self. Physicians like Jon Kabat-Zinn and Herbert Benson introduced medicine to mindfulness by empirically establishing the healing effects on the body of breathing, meditating and "de-stressing." Besel van der Kolk (1996, 2014) taught therapists that the *body* becomes the repository for trauma memories when original events so overwhelm the brain that it loses its ability to encode in words and sequential narrative; to reach the patient's experience we must include his body in the treatment process. Dan Siegel (2007, 2010) became one of the more influential spokespeople for folding mindfulness into psychotherapy because he spent time explaining how to fold neuroscience into mindfulness. Porges and his colleagues (Geller & Porges, 2014; Porges & Dana, 2018) emphasize "therapeutic presence," the need for therapists to learn how to be psycho-physiologically still and present for their patient's sake.

Therapeutic presence is being grounded in one's healthy integrated self; being open, receptive, and absorbed in what is taking place right now; and having an expanded sense of awareness and perception (Geller & Porges, 2014). This is the same awareness about which we spoke in Chapter 3. It is a way of experiencing, a whole mind-body state. It is internal to the therapist, not an externally wielded technique. It requires daily attention to develop into a life practice. As therapists, we need this ability to be able to feel the uncontrollable, instantaneous fight or flight or freeze responses that flame through us when a patient does or says something unsettling and transform this reactivity into a stillness that elongates time long enough to allow us to reach compassion. When our patients hurt, they are at risk for hurting us; when they are riled, if we are empathic we feel riled too. If we are caught off guard, we are likely to feel jolted and defensive. In the real-time of real therapy when we are personally provoked, compassion doesn't just appear. It takes caring attention to work toward compassion, humility, and personal responsibility; they aren't just in us because we've learned they are important. The transference/countertransference model helps us get there by encouraging us to look within for private emotional upsets that may be heating up our defensiveness and clouding our perception. The therapeutic presence model helps us get there by teaching us to move inside our bodies to settle our heart-rate, breathing, and brain waves. When we physically calm ourselves, we feel safer, which helps us feel more confident, which helps us access our senses and knowledge more effectively. The result is we can reflect on a moment of rupture even as we are feeling it; we can speak with our patient respectfully without shading our words unconsciously with hostility or dismissal. This is why the rupture repair model chose to include mindfulness in their training for repairing ruptures.

There is a second aspect to therapeutic presence that is relevant to frictions arising in the first place. Whenever we tense, withdraw, or become agitated our patient senses a threat and closes down. In contrast, if we remain open, calm, and present, our patient detects social safety. Sensing social safety autonomically triggers what Porges' polyvagal theory calls the mammalian vagal circuit of social engagement which helps strengthen trust, problem solving, and brain plasticity (Hope & Sugarman, 2015; see Chapter 5). The social engagement neural circuitry activates calm interest, open receptivity, curious absorption, and emotional and mental spontaneity, rather than narrowed, hypervigilant scanning, tense rigidity, and shutting down.

Supervision

The second training ground for therapists who want to feel more confident working with upsets in the relationship is supervision. You want a supervisor who gives you immediate feedback so you get as near as can be to a hands-on, sensory feel for what you just did that hurt your patient. You want a supervisor who invites you to connect what he saw, with what you felt inside, so you can learn to recognize your own signals; one who teaches you how to test your feelings against observable data; and one who models how to tolerate and integrate contradictions rather than explaining away one observation or the other.

This may mean a supervisor in the room with you or watching remotely (Feinstein, 2020; Feinstein & Yager, 2013; Feinstein et al., 2015). It may mean videotaping sessions and watching them with your supervisor, pausing to understand key moments (Eubanks et al., 2019). It may mean using audio recordings to capture sequence, exact words, and tone. It's impossible to report from memory what we don't know to look for, can't see in ourselves, or can't word. The most upsetting moments in therapy are the most difficult to narrate; they are complex, hold more feelings than words, and usually blow through the room in a way that upends and confuses. It helps to see things through another person's eyes, particularly when that person is more experienced or feels less personally vulnerable than we might. If supervision days later is all that is available, then take notes immediately following a session, attending most to sequence, quotations, and nonverbal process both from your patient and inside you.

Working with relational issues in psychotherapy also requires supervision that opens room for discussion of the therapist's feelings because the therapist is 50% of the relationship. This kind of supervision is sacred space and requires skill on the part of the supervisor; a supervisee's feelings need to be treated respectfully and understood as data and as *information critical to understanding the process* (see Bram, 2010, 2013, 2015), not as opportunities to turn supervision into psychotherapy. The supervisor can always suggest the supervisee take up particular issues in his personal therapy, but it is never appropriate to slip into personal therapy-like dynamics in supervision. Trust is key and it is earned through the supervisor's maintenance of collegial boundaries while being able to hear deeply personal responses. As Eubanks et al. (2019) put it, "Ruptures can be emotionally challenging experiences for therapists, so supervisors need to build a strong supervisory alliance to create a safe space for trainees to share and explore their experiences of ruptures" (p. 572).

Finally, part of learning how to use our feelings as information is learning what Erik Erikson (1957/1964) called disciplined subjectivity; namely, how to calibrate intuition with objectivity rather than throw one or the other out. Gut feelings ("I just had a feeling that was what he was thinking," or "I could just tell she was feeling contempt") can be invaluable data *but only if* we vet their credibility and create hypotheses from them that can be tested ("What is the data for that? Was it something she said, how she looked?" and, "What is your confidence level for that inference?"). Rather than call all "impressions" inherently unreliable, learn how to establish your accuracy (Bram & Peebles, 2014, pp. 31–54; Peebles-Kleiger, 2002), your blind spots, and the degree to which you tend to over-amplify (or miss) particular kinds of signals.

Therapy for the Therapist

Personal therapy is the third piece for developing an ability to recover and think clearly when you are provoked by your patient or discover yourself provoking them. No single research group has dug into the process of replication and refinement of design over time on this topic the way Strupp's or Safran's and Muran's groups did on alliance and ruptures. However, there are consistent trends.

Therapists interviewed about how personal therapy affected their work reported being able to be more human and patient and being able to empathize and pace the work better because they understood what it's like to be a patient (Macran et al., 1999). They reported being better able to work at a deeper emotional level, to separate their feelings from their patient's feelings, and to be less judgmental because they had become less judgmental of themselves. They were able to know their blind spots, to give their patients space to respond and grapple without jumping in too quickly, and to partner more mutually rather than hierarchically because, as Harry Stack Sullivan (1953) said, "Everyone is much more simply human than otherwise."

Their descriptions converge with studies of therapists rated by peers to be "master therapists" (Bennett-Levy, 2019). These individuals were "voracious learners, curious, reflective, and valued cognitive complexity and ambiguity; they were emotionally receptive, self-aware, non-defensive and open to feedback" (Bennett-Levy, 2019, p. 136). Most importantly for our purposes, they sought out personal therapy.

In contrast, Ackerman & Hilsenroth's (2001) review of studies of therapists receiving low alliance and rupture-repair ratings found these therapists to be rigid, self-focused, aloof, distracted, tense, defensive, bored, blaming, or belittling. They were inflexible and over structuring of the therapy, used inappropriate self-disclosure, relentlessly interpreted a patient's feelings toward them as being a product of other past relationships, inappropriately used silence, and made superficial interventions when deeper emotional connection was needed. Such behaviors are characteristic of people who are having difficulty with: deeper emotions, having enough mental space available to concentrate steadily on their patients, and being empathic. Personal therapy would help address such personal struggles. Paula Heimann (1950) thought so too, explaining that personal therapy helps a therapist know, understand, and tolerate his difficult feelings so that "he will not impute to his patient what belongs to himself" (p. 83). The more complex and relationally distressed a patient is, the more a therapist's personality traits matter (Moe & Thimm, 2021).

If you want to maximize learning how to navigate those stuck places that come from inside the relationship with your patients, don't be afraid to choose a therapy and a therapist that tackle the deep issues and the rough emotions. You'll want a therapist who is himself steady emotionally, who can engage with you in an emotionally involved way without losing sight of you or losing hold of the healthy boundaries of therapy. He needs to be able to own his mistakes, because how he does so will model for you how to do so with your own patients. And finally, if you can, find someone who understands how we split off aspects of ourselves out of shame or guilt. You want to be able to meet and greet all aspects of yourself and bring them back into the fold of the person that is you. You and your patient will be blindsided less frequently by your darker side if you do.

Self-Care

None of our effort to learn will hold traction as therapists if we don't make self-care a lifetime practice. Self-care extends over several domains: physical, emotional, social, financial, and spiritual. "Health" means maintaining enough balance, flexibility, range of motion, and strength to establish and re-establish repeatedly that sweet hum of stability and well-being that Csikszentmihalyi (1990) calls flow. We are delicate ecosystems. What, how much, and how frequently we eat, hydrate, and sleep determines how much information our frontal lobes can hold and reflect upon, how easily those frontal connections are able to slow the fires of reactivity, and how flexible and resilient we're able to be. The depth and richness of our friend networks steady our heart rate and make us less anxious and more patient. Living beneath our financial means in an organized way lowers the background stress of money worries, stress that erodes our ability to concentrate and enjoy delivering therapy. Taking time to contemplate our personal reasons for doing this work and for being alive creates meaning in life and work, meaning that acts as a spiritual compass during times that seem to make no sense. The stability of health in our delicate ecosystem is a dynamic, continuously reconfiguring, alive process that asks for daily attention and lifelong practice to maintain.

Let us move now to considering more deeply the matter of spiritual health and the creating of meaning.

References

Ackerman, S.J., & Hilsenroth, M.J. (2001). A review of therapist characteristics and techniques negatively impacting the therapeutic alliance. *Psychotherapy*, 38(2), 171–185.

Adverse Childhood Experiences. (n.d.). Centers for Disease Control and Prevention (CDC). Retrieved April 6, 2021. https://www.cdc.gov/violenceprevention/acestudy/about.html

Ardito, R.B., & Rabellino, D. (2011). Therapeutic alliance and outcome of psychotherapy: Historical excursus, measurements, and prospects for research. *Frontiers in Psychology*, 2(Article 270).

Banyai, E., Meszaros, I., & Csokay, L. (1982). Interaction between hypnotist and subject: A social psychophysiologic approach (preliminary report). In D. Waxman, P.C. Misra, M. Gibson, & M.A. Basker (Eds.), *Modern trends in hypnosis* (pp. 97–108). Boston, MA: Springer.

Bateson, G., Jackson, D., Haley, J., & Weakland, J. (1956), Toward a theory of schizophrenia. *Behavioral Science*, 1(4), 251–264.

Benedetti, F. (2011). *The patient's brain: The neuroscience behind the doctor-patient relationship*. New York, NY: Oxford University Press.

Benedetti, F. (2013). Placebo and the new physiology of the doctor-patient relationship. *Physiological Reviews*, 93(3), 1207–1246.

Benedetti, F. (2014a). Placebo effects: From the neurobiological paradigm to translational implications. *Neuron*, 84(3), 623–637.

Benedetti, F. (2014b). *Understanding placebo effects: Understanding the mechanisms in health and disease* (Second ed.). Oxford, UK: Oxford University Press.

Bennett-Levy, J. (2019). Why therapists should walk the talk: The theoretical and empirical case for personal practice in therapist training and professional development. *Journal of Behavior Therapy and Experimental Psychiatry*, 62, 133–145.

Benson, H. (1997). The nocebo effect: History and physiology. *Preventive Medicine*, 26(5 Pt 1), 612–615.

Bergin, A.E. (1966). Some implications of psychotherapy for therapeutic practice. *Journal of Abnormal Psychology*, 71(4), 235–246.

Berkman, L.F., & Syme, S.L. (1979). Social networks, host resistance, and mortality: A nine-year follow-up study of Alameda County residents. *American Journal of Epidemiology*, 109(2), 186–204.

Binder, J.L., & Strupp, H.H. (1997). "Negative process": A recurrently discovered and underestimated facet of therapeutic process and outcome in the individual psychotherapy of adults. *Clinical Psychology: Science and Practice*, 4(2), 121–139.

Bordin, E.S. (1979). The generalizability of the psychoanalytic concept of the working alliance. *Psychotherapy: Theory, Research and Practice*, 16(3), 252–260.

Bram, A.D. (2010). The relevance of the Rorschach and patient-examiner relationship in treatment planning and outcome assessment. *Journal of Personality Assessment*, 92(2), 91–115.

Bram, A.D. (2013). Psychological testing and treatment implications: We can say more. *Journal of Personality Assessment*, 95(4), 319–331.

Bram, A.D. (2015). To resume a stalled psychotherapy? Psychological testing to understand an impasse and reevaluate treatment options. *Journal of Personality Assessment*, 97(3), 241–249.

Bram, A.D., & Peebles, M.J. (2014). *Psychological testing that matters: Creating a road map for effective treatment*. Washington, DC: American Psychological Association.

Brazelton, T.B., Tronick, E., Adamson, L., Als, H., & Wise, S. (1975). Early mother-infant reciprocity. *Ciba Foundation Symposium*, 33, 137–154.

Buber, M. (1970). *I and thou* (W. Kaufman, trans.). New York, NY: Simon and Schuster. (Original work published 1923)

Castonguay, L.G., Boswell, J.F., Constantino, M.J., Goldfried, M.R., & Hill, C.E. (2010). Training implications of harmful effects of psychological treatments. *American Psychologist*, 65(1), 34–49.

Conboy, B.T., Brooks, R., Meltzoff, A.N., & Kuhl, P.K. (2015). Social interaction in infants' learning of second-language phonetics: An exploration of brain-behavior relations. *Developmental Neuropsychology*, 40(4), 216–229.

Crandall, F.M. (1897). Editorial. *Archives of Pediatrics*, 14(6), 448–454.

Csikszentmihalyi, M. (1990). *Flow: The psychology of optimal experience*. New York, NY: Harper & Row, Publishers.

Derra, C., & Schwab, R. (2013). Analgesics in the context of the doctor-patient relationship. *Die Medizinische Welt*, 65(6), 317–321.

DiJulio, B., Hamel, L., Munana, C., & Brodie, M. (2018). *Loneliness and social isolation in the United States, the United Kingdom, and Japan: An international survey*. Kaiser Family Foundation. https://www.kff.org/other/report/loneliness-and-social-isolation-in-the-united-states-the-united-kingdom-and-japan-an-international-survey/

Dikker, S., Wan, L., Davidesco, I., Kaggen, L., Oostrik, M., McClintock, J., Rowland, J., Michalareas, G., Van Bavel, J.J., Ding, M., & Poeppel, D. (2017). Brain-to-brain synchrony tracks real-world dynamic group interactions in the classroom. *Current Biology*, 27(9), 1375–1380.

Egbert, L.D., & Jackson, S.H. (2013). Therapeutic benefit of the anesthesiologist-patient relationship. *Anesthesiology*, 119(6), 1465–1468.

Ehret, M.J., & Wang, M. (2013). How to increase medication adherence: What works? *Mental Health Clinician*, 2(8), 230–232.

Erikson, E. (1957/1964), The nature of clinical evidence. In *Insight and responsibility* (pp. 47–80). New York, NY: W.W. & Company.

Eubanks, C.F., Muran, J.C., & Safran, J.D. (2019). Repairing alliance ruptures. In J.C. Norcross & M.J. Lambert (Eds.), *Psychotherapy relationships that work: Evidence-based therapist contributions* (3rd ed., Vol 1, pp. 549–579). New York, NY: Oxford University Press.

Evers, A.W.M., Colloca, L., Blease, C., Annoni, M., Atlas, L.Y., Benedetti, F., Bingel, U., Buche, C., Carvalho, C., Colagiuri, B., Crum, A.J., Enck, P., Gaab, J., Geers, A.L., Howick, J., Jensen, K.B., Kirsch, I., Meissner, K., Napadow, V.,… Kelley, J.M. (2018). Implications of placebo and nocebo effects for clinical practice: Expert consensus. *Psychotherapy and Psychosomatics, 87*(4), 204–210.

Fatollahzade, M., Parvizi, S., Kashaki, M., Haghani, H., & Alinejad, M. (2020, April 21). The effect of gentle human touch during endotracheal suctioning on procedural pain response in preterm infant neonatal intensive care units: A randomized controlled crossover study. *Journal of Maternal-Fetal and Neonatal Medicine, 51,* 155–164. 10.1080/14767058.2020.1755649

Feinstein, R.E. (2020). Descriptions and reflections on the cognitive apprenticeship model of psychotherapy training & supervision. *Journal of Contemporary Psychotherapy, 51,* 155–164. 10.1007/s10879-020-09480-6

Feinstein, R.E., Huhn, R., & Yager, J. (2015). Apprenticeship model of psychotherapy training and supervision: Utilizing six tools of experiential learning. *Academic Psychiatry, 39*(5), 585–589.

Feinstein, R.E., & Yager, J. (2013). Advanced psychotherapy training: Psychotherapy scholars' track, and the apprenticeship model. *Academic Psychiatry, 37*(4), 248–253.

Felitti, V.J., Anda, R.F., Nordenberg, D., Williamson, D.F., Spitz, A.M., Edwards, V., Koss, M.P., & Marks, J.S. (1998). Relationship of childhood abuse and household dysfunction to many of the leading causes of death in adults: The Adverse Childhood Experiences (ACE) study. *American Journal of Preventive Medicine, 14*(4), 245–258.

Gabbard, G.O. (1991). Technical approaches to transference hate in the analysis of borderline patients. *International Journal of Psycho-analysis, 72*(Pt 4), 625–637.

Gardner, H. (1983). *Frames of mind: The theory of multiple intelligences.* New York, NY: Basic Books.

Gardner, J.R., Lipner, L.M., Eubanks, C.F., & Muran, J.C. (2020). A therapist's guide to repairing ruptures in the working alliance. In J.N. Fuertes (Ed.), *Working alliance skills for mental health professionals* (pp. 159–180). New York, NY: Oxford University Press.

Geller, S., & Porges, S.W. (2014). Therapeutic presence: Neurophysiological mechanisms mediating feeling safe in therapeutic relationships. *Journal of Psychotherapy Integration, 24*(3), 178–192.

Geri, T., Viceconti, A., Marco, M., Testa, M., & Rossettini, G. (2019). Manual therapy: Exploiting the role of human touch. *Musculoskeletal Science and Practice, 44,* Article 102044.

Gottman, J.M. (1994). *What predicts divorce? The relationship between marital processes and marital outcomes.* Hillsdale, NJ: Lawrence Erlbaum.

Graff, T., Luke, S.G., & Birmingham, W. (2019). Supportive hand-holding attenuates pupillary responses to stress in adult couples. *PLoS One, 14*(2), 1–20.

Ham, J., & Tronick, E. (2009). Relational psychophysiology: Lessons from mother–infant physiology research on dyadically expanded states of consciousness. *Psychotherapy Research, 19*(6), 619–632.

Hanh, T.N. (1975). *The miracle of mindfulness.* (M. Ho, trans.). Boston MA: Beacon Press. (Original work published 1974)

Hannan, C., Lambert, M.J., Harmon, C., Nielsen, S.L., Smart, D.W., Shimokawa, K., & Sutton, S.W. (2005). A lab test and algorithms for identifying clients at risk for treatment failure. *Journal of Clinical Psychology, 61*(2), 155–163.

Heimann, P. (1950). On counter-transference. *International Journal of Psycho-Analysis, 31*, 81–84.

Herrington, C. & Chiodo, L.M. (2014). Human touch effectively and safely reduces pain in the newborn intensive care unit. *Pain Management Nursing: Official Journal of the American Society of Pain Management Nurses, 15*(1), 107–115.

Hoff, B. (1982). *The tao of pooh.* New York, NY: Penguin Books.

Holt, R.R. (2002). Quantitative research on the primary process: Method and findings. *Journal of the American Psychoanalytic Association, 50*(2), 457–482.

Holt-Lunstad, J., Smith, T.B., Baker, M., Harris, T., & Stephenson, D. (2015). Loneliness and social isolation as risk factors for mortality: A meta-analytic review. *Perspectives on Psychological Science, 10*(2), 227–237.

Holt-Lunstad, J., Smith, T.B., & Layton, J.B. (2010). Social relationships and mortality risk: A meta-analytic review. *PLoS Med, 7*(July 27). 10.1371/journal.pmed.1000316

Hope, A.E., & Sugarman, L.I. (2015). Orienting hypnosis. *American Journal of Clinical Hypnosis, 57*(3), 212–229.

Horwitz, L. (1983). Projective identification in dyads and groups. *International Journal of Group Psychotherapy, 33*(3), 259–279.

Housman, J. & Dorman, S. (2005). The Alameda County study: A systematic chronological review. *American Journal of Health Education, 36*(5), 302–308.

Iacoboni, M. (2008). *Mirroring people: The science of empathy and how we connect with others.* New York, NY: Farrar, Straus and Giroux.

Julius R.J., Novitsky, M.A., & Dubin, W. R. (2009). Medication adherence: A review of the literature and implications for clinical practice. *Journal of Psychiatric Practice, 15*(1), 34–44.

Kuhl, P.K., Tsao, F., & Liu, H. (2003). Foreign-language experience in infancy: Effects of short-term exposure and social interaction on phonetic learning. *Proceedings of the National Academy of Sciences, 100*(15), 9096–9101.

Lambert, M.J. (2010). *Prevention of treatment failure: The use of measuring, monitoring, and feedback in clinical practice.* Washington, DC: American Psychological Association.

Lambert, M.J., Whipple, J.L., & Kleinstauber, M. (2018). Collecting and delivering progress feedback: A meta-analysis of routine outcome monitoring. *Psychotherapy, 55*(4), 520–537.

Lambert, M.J., Whipple, J.L., Vermeersch, D.A., Smart, D.W., Hawkins, E.J., Nielsen, S.L., & Goates, M. (2002). Enhancing psychotherapy outcomes via providing feedback on client progress: A replication. *Clinical Psychology and Psychotherapy, 9*(2), 91–103.

Lazar, S. (2001). Knowing, influencing, and healing: Paranormal phenomena and implications for psychoanalysis and psychotherapy. *Psychoanalytic Inquiry* 21(1), 113–131.

Linton, P.H., Travis, R.P., Kuechenmeister, C.A., & White, H. (1977). Correlation between heart rate covariation, personality and hypnotic state. *American Journal of Clinical Hypnosis*, 19(3), 148–154.

Lipner, L.M., Liu, D., & Muran, J.C. (2019). Getting on the same page: Introducing alliance rupture as a path to mutual empathy and change in psychotherapy. In A. Foster & Z. Yaseen (Eds.), *Teaching empathy in healthcare* (117–126). Cham, Switzerland: Springer.

Lytle, R., Garcia-Sierra, A., & Kuhl, P.K. (2018). Two are better than one: Infant language learning from video improves in the presence of peers. *Proceedings of the National Academy of Sciences*, 115(40), 9859–9866.

Macran, S., Stiles, W.B., & Smith, J.A. (1999). How does personal therapy affect therapists' practice. *Journal of Counseling Psychology*, 46(4), 419–431.

Mayer, E.L. (2001). On "telepathic dreams?": An unpublished paper by Robert J. Stoller. *Journal of the American Psychoanalytic Association*, 49(2), 629–657.

Mayer, E.L. (2007). *Extraordinary knowing: Science, skepticism, and the inexplicable powers of the human mind*. New York, NY: Bantam Books.

McGilchrist, I. (2009). *The master and his emissary*. New Haven, CT: Yale University Press.

Miglioretti, M., Mariani, F., & Vecchio, L. (2018). Could patient engagement promote a health system free from malpractice litigation risk? In Information Resources Management Association (Ed.), *Health economics and healthcare reform: Breakthroughs in research and practice* (pp. 431–454). Hershey, PA: IGI Global.

Moe, F.D., & Thimm, J. (2021). Personal therapy and the personal therapist. *Nordic Psychology*, 73(1), 3–28. 10.1080/19012276.2020.1762713.

Moore, P.J., Adler, N.E., & Robertson, P.A. (2000). Medical malpractice: The effect of doctor-patient relations on medical patient perceptions and malpractice intentions. *Western Journal of Medicine*, 173(4), 244–250.

Moss, T., & Gengerelli, J.A. (1967). Telepathy and emotional stimuli: A controlled experiment. *Journal of Abnormal Psychology*, 72(4), 341–348.

Moss, T., & Gengerelli, J.A. (1970). ESP effects generated by affective states. *Behavioral Neuropsychiatry*, 2(9–10), 8–12.

Nakano, S., Sugahara, H., Sakamoto, M., Ozeki, T., Uemura, N., Nyu, S., Sunami, Y., Matsuki, S., & Umetsuki, M. (1998). Factors influencing placebo effects in patients with psychosomatic disorders: Doctor-patient relationship, patient's motivation and expectation for drug therapy. *Japanese Journal of Clinical Pharmacology and Therapeutics*, 30(1), 1–7.

Oliver, M. (2016). *Upstream: Selected essays*. New York, NY: Penguin Press.

Peebles, M.J. (2012). *Beginnings: The art and science of planning psychotherapy* (2nd ed.). New York, NY: Routledge Press.

Peebles, M.J. (2018). Harm in hypnosis: Three understandings from psychoanalysis that can help. *American Journal of Clinical Hypnosis*, 60(3), 239–261.

Peebles-Kleiger, M.J. (2002). Elaboration of some sequence analysis strategies: Examples and guidelines for level of confidence. *Journal of Personality Assessment*, 79(1), 19–38.

Piazza, E.A., Hasenfratz, L., Hasson, U., & Lew-Williams, C. (2020). Infant and adult brains are coupled to the dynamics of natural communication. *Association for Psychological Science*, 31(1), 6–17.

Porges, S., & Dana, D. (Eds.). (2018). *Clinical applications of the polyvagal theory: The emergence of polyvagal-informed therapies*. New York, NY: W.W. Norton & Company, Inc.

Racker, H. (1957). The meanings and uses of countertransference. *Psychoanalytic Quarterly*, 26(3), 303–357.

Reik, T. (1948). *Listening with the third ear: The inner experience of a psychoanalyst*. New York, NY: Farrar, Straus and Giroux.

Rogers, C. (1961). *On becoming a person: A therapist's view of psychotherapy*. New York, NY: Houghton Mifflin Harcourt Publishing Company.

Rogers, C. (1980). *A way of being*. New York, NY: Houghton Mifflin Company.

Sartre, J. (1958). *No exit* (P. Bowles, trans.). New York, NY: Samuel French, Inc. (Original work published 1945)

Schore, A.N. (1994). *Affect regulation and the origin of the self: Neurobiology of emotional development*. Hillsdale, NJ: Lawrence Erlbaum Associates, Publishers.

Schore, A.N. (2009). Right-brain affect regulation: An essential mechanism of development, trauma, dissociation, and psychotherapy. In D. Fosha, D. J. Siegel, & M. Solomon (Eds.), *The healing power of emotion: Affective neuroscience, development, and clinical practice* (pp. 112–144). New York, NY: W.W. Norton & Company.

Schulman, M. & Maul, A. (2019, February). Screening for adverse childhood experiences and trauma. Center for health care strategies. https://www.chcs.org/media/TA-Tool-Screening-for-ACEs-and-Trauma_020619.pdf

Searles, H. (1979). The patient as therapist to his analyst. In *Countertransference and related subjects: Selected papers* (pp. 380–459). New York, NY: International Universities Press. (Original work published 1975)

Siegel, D.J. (2007). *The mindful brain: Reflection and attunement in the cultivation of well-being*. New York, NY: W.W. Norton & Company, Inc.

Siegel, D.J. (2010). *The mindful therapist: A clinician's guide to mindsight and neural integration*. New York, NY: W.W. Norton & Company, Inc.

Spitz, R.A. (1945). Hospitalism: An inquiry into the genesis of psychiatric conditions in early childhood. *Psychoanalytic Study of the Child*, 1(1), 53–74.

Strupp, H.H. (1980). Success and failure in time-limited psychotherapy. Further evidence (Comparison 4). *Archives of General Psychiatry*, 37(8), 947–954.

Sullivan, H.S. (1953). *Conceptions of modern psychiatry: The First William Alanson White Memorial Lectures*. New York, NY: W.W. Norton & Co.

Tronick, E. (2001). Emotional connections and dyadic consciousness in infant-mother and patient-therapist interactions: Commentary on paper by Frank M. Lachmann. *Psychoanalytic Dialogues*, 11(2), 187–194

Tronick, E. (2007). *The neurobehavioral and social emotional development of infants and children*. New York, NY: W.W. Norton & Company.

Tronick, E., Als, H., Adamson, L., Wise, S., & Brazelton, T.B. (1978). The infant's response to entrapment between contradictory messages in face-to-face interaction. *Journal of the American Academy of Child psychiatry*, 17(1), 1–13.

Trumble, S.C., O'Brien, M.L., O'Brien, M., & Hartwig, B. (2006). Communication skills training for doctors increases patient satisfaction. *Clinical Governance: An International Journal, 11*(4), 299–307.

Tufte, E.R. (1983). *The visual display of quantitative information.* Cheshire, CT: Graphics Press.

Tufte, E.R. (2006). *Beautiful evidence.* Cheshire, CT: Graphics Press.

UMass Boston. (2009, November 30). Still face experiment: Dr. Edward Tronick [Video file]. Youtube. https://www.youtube.com/watch?v=apzXGEbZht0

Umberson, D., & Montez, J.K., (2010). Social relationships and health: A flashpoint for health policy. *Journal of Health and Social Behavior, 51*(1 suppl), S54–S66.

van der Kolk, B. (1996). The body keeps the score: Approaches to the psychobiology of posttraumatic stress disorder. In B. van der Kolk, A. McFarlane, & L. Weisaeth (Eds.), *Traumatic stress: The effects of overwhelming experience on mind, body, and society* (pp. 214–241). New York, NY: Guilford Press.

van der Kolk, B. (2014). *The body keeps the score: Mind, brain and body in the transformation of trauma.* London, UK: Penguin.

Velligan D.I., Weiden, P.J., Sajatovic, M., Scott, J., Carpenter, D., Ross, R., & Docherty, J.P. (2009). The expert consensus guideline series: Adherence problems in patients with serious and persistent mental illness. *Journal of Clinical Psychiatry, 70*(suppl. 4), 1–48.

Virshup, B.B., Oppenberg, A.A., & Coleman, M.M. (1999). Strategic risk management: Reducing malpractice claims through more effective doctor-patient communication. *American Journal of Medical Quality, 14*(4), 153–159.

Wass, S.V., Noreika, V., Georgieva, S., Clackson, K., Brightman, L., Nutbrown, R., Covarrubias, L.S., & Leong, V. (2018). Parental neural responsivity to infants' visual attention: How mature brains influence immature brains during social interaction. *PLoS Biology, 16*(12), 1–18.

Winnicott, D.W. (1949). Hate in the counter-transference. *International Journal of Psycho-Analysis, 30*(Pt 2), 69–74.

Winnicott, D.W. (1953). Transitional objects and transitional phenomena: A study of the first not-me possession. *International Journal of Psycho-Analysis, 34*(Pt 2), 89–97.

Wright, K. (2016). Social networks, interpersonal social support, and health outcomes: A health communication perspective. *Frontiers in Communication, 1*(Article 10). 10.3389/fcomm.2016.00010

Zilcha-Mano, S., Eubanks, C.F., Bloch-Elkouby, S., & Muran, J.C. (2020). Can we agree we just had a rupture? Patient-therapist congruence on ruptures and its effects on outcome in brief relational therapy versus cognitive-behavioral therapy. *Journal of Counseling Psychology, 67*(3), 315–325.

7 Creating Meaning

> In racing they say that your car goes where your eyes go.
> —Garth Stein, *The Art of Racing in the Rain*

The vitality of psychotherapy fades when the patient, or we, lose touch with why we are doing the work. Without a greater purpose psychotherapy risks feeling vapid or stuck. Near the end of his 96 years, the great cellist, Pablo Casals (1970), reflected, "One must, of course, master technique; at the same time, one must not become enslaved by it—one must understand that *the purpose of technique is to transmit the inner meaning*, the message, of the music" (p. 76, emphasis added). As psychotherapists, we want to be aware of where we are directing our wider gaze as we listen and intervene. We want to appreciate how our personal sensitivity to meaning and purpose—or its absence—infuses our techniques. When we do so we can help our patient do the same.

Exhaustion and Discouragement: "Why Keep Trying?"

Everyone faces discouragement. Perhaps our brother dies; perhaps we have cancer; perhaps despite our best efforts in therapy we feel frightened again or our marriage falls apart. The rise and fall of our spirits is as inevitable as the tides. To live life bravely requires an anchor, a place to return to that is internal and transcendent, that reminds us why we continue to persist. We call this centering place our values, purpose, or meaning.

Ellen worked hard at therapy but despite her determination, the embedded harshness of her grandmother kept emerging from her in barbed comments. As if her Sisyphean internal task of softening that harshness weren't enough, now her husband had been diagnosed with Alzheimers. In our session, Ellen felt confused. It was as if her mind were filled with noise; her body prickled, on guard against getting hurt, but by what she didn't know. She described finding herself being bubbly and fizzy in conversations with friends, trying to keep people laughing so nothing bad would happen, meanwhile flagellating herself on the inside for perceived mistakes.

DOI: 10.4324/9781315449043-7

"As we get older, we keep losing more of what we had," I shared. "How do we keep growing in the face of that? What is important to you, Ellen? What brings you joy? How are you valuable?" Ellen was quiet, unsure, but her eyes stayed on mine ready to listen.

Claire's only sibling, a brother, died. She handled all funeral arrangements and estate problems. In our sessions, she spoke little of his death. Instead, she reported she "felt crappy since I came back from Italy. It's like a sense of gloom that changes lighter and darker, but it's still gloom. It's like a morass. I keep thinking the same thoughts over and over. I'm just trying to ride it out."

I listened as she struggled to put her finger on her mood. She talked about a dissatisfying book club gathering, of a program she'd initiated at her former job that had been dismantled, of a monthly lunch gathering that was missing two women who were too ill to attend.

"I think that since your brother died, you've been faced with end-of-life feelings, like "Do I matter" "What's the point?"

Claire became irritated. "Those questions are too big. I don't know how to begin to think about them."

"Well, why do you think we're all here?"

"I don't know. I guess I believe there's a unifying force in the universe because everything is so miraculous. But I don't see any reason for me being alive."

"How do you reconcile those two things—that there is a unifying force, but no reason for you being here?"

Claire shifted uncomfortably. "I can't think. I don't know."

"That's ok. It's not something you need to *know* exactly. It's just that I think that the 'loneliness' and 'discouragement' you've been telling me about really isn't depression creeping in again. I think you're searching for meaning since Arnie died. That's not easy. It's something we all need to do at some point, but it takes time, and thinking. It's not an 'answer' we need to find; it's an understanding that we cobble together."

Ester was 79; her cancer had returned a third time. Gritty determination was her hallmark, but now her spark was dimmed. She had always sought the best doctors from the best hospitals, but lately, she didn't have her old energy to hammer her doctors with questions or the same incisiveness of thinking for cutting through their answers. A question hung heavy in our room: what was her reason for fighting? When I named this, Ester reared up. Her response was troubled and troubling. "Maybe I should change my attitude to 'I can't recover to where I was before,' but *I refuse to accept that.* If only I work harder I can get there. Dying terrifies me—I'll be gone forever. Everything else goes on and I will not."

Ester swung back at herself: "But what if every day is a chronic disappointment? There's always something wrong, with everything. There are too many details to track; I can't do it. I feel like I recover then

I'm slapped down again. What's the point? I have no idea of the point of the world. There is more misery than joy. What do you think the purpose of the world is?"

I have been surprised by how few people intentionally think about why they are alive and what their purpose is for being here. I have been startled and saddened by people who adamantly refuse to go there, even when I offer to go there with them. I've noticed that patients with failing health, coupled with either dwindling financial resources or meager relational resources have little reserve for picturing the prospects of why. If their background also held trauma and/or their lifetime coping strategies have been to inflate their self-esteem by perceiving themselves as better than others, by holding power, or carrying social clout, it becomes impossible. They crumple in on the hollowness of their spiritual core. Meaning needs to be thought about early in life so its roots thicken and embed in our actions, forming a core that supports us when we are blindsided by life.

Growth May Not Always Feel Positive

It is not just losses in the twilight of life that call out for meaning; growth itself can. Change does not always feel good, at least not right away. Changing oneself can bring loss of friends, even family members, as people respond to our new way of relating with discomfort. They want us to be like we were before. Change challenges us in ways we did not expect and now have to contend with.

Neala was raised in a household afflicted by alcoholism and verbal cruelty. Although her inner nature was sensitive, expressing empathy and vulnerability had proven to be unsafe. To survive, she became tough. Her anger became a shield; her tongue a sharp weapon. She had needed to anticipate attack and throw verbal punches. We worked painstakingly to unpack each angry outburst until Neala could slow down her fight response enough to look before yelling. However, instead of feeling proud of what she was accomplishing, Neala felt distress. Why? Because now that she was slowing down enough to feel her inside reactions to things people said, powerlessness, fear, and uncertainty seeped into her gut. These sensations were what her toughness had been protecting her against. This discovery of buried pain crushed her. "So much more work to do," she wept. I listened and sat with her. We sat quietly with the truth of what she was saying. Slowly I helped her look around and pick through what to her felt like emotional rubble to re-discover the reasons she was working determinedly to rebuild her life differently.

Patients seldom name "meaning" as the issue with which they want help. It is up to us to name it, and when we do so, we need to be prepared for the possibility that they might ask us why we feel the work of living and growing are worth doing.

Transport and Transaction

There is a continuum in any human relationship spanning from transaction to transport. At the transaction end, people exchange currency for goods. For example, a patient may want to relate to us by paying a fee to acquire a skill; someone aspiring toward social mobility may trade information for popularity or flattery to acquire access. In transactions, time is a commodity and dictates interchanges. On the transport end, people seek being, becoming, and transcending; for example, sharing energy to expand into more than each were before. On the transport end, experience is relevant, not time. Therapists and patients vary on where on that continuum they are comfortable engaging as individuals. They will vary as well in how comfortable they are being at either end with each other.

Joseph Campbell had the visionary's gift for piercing the fog of differences among religious and mythical stories from various times and continents and seeing into their common core (Campbell et al., 1988). To him, myths represented humankind's recurring quest for truths about the mysteries in life. One motif he described was the "mystical journey." The mystical journey is considered sacred. When an opportunity for a mystical journey opens for people, some feel beckoned; others recoil. In the mystical journey, one loosens engagement with the material world and moves consciousness inward or beyond to an un-wordable realm. This journey propels the traveler into darkness before light appears. Stumbling through darkness and unknown is unnerving, disruptive, and unsettling, so much so that in the stories of mystical journey there is a guide and rituals to facilitate the crossing. The outcome of this story is an expansion of consciousness, an awareness of more complexity and dimensions than previously realized, and mental transformation.

Psychotherapy presents the opportunity for a mystical journey, however brief its encounter or modest the epiphanies. To open up this opportunity we need to open ourselves to interacting more than transactionally with our patient. Being able to do so and stay within the boundaries and therapeutic frame of therapy requires training. Therapists who don't secure such training may feel threatened or seduced by the emotional intimacy of moving beyond transaction. Both these reactions cause problems for patients. There are benefits for patients of therapists who take the time to master the process of therapeutic intimacy. Transport is catalytic (Lewis, 2014). Its energy propels the mind-body-brain into reorganization in the same way that the startle of the orienting response opens a neurological portal into brain plasticity (Hope & Sugarman, 2015). Moreover, a patient's behavioral changes are more likely to sustain themselves past the end of the formal psychotherapy sessions if authentic connection occurs between therapist and patient (Aftab, 2020; Shedler, 2010). Such connection is transformative.

We cannot orchestrate transport in psychotherapy. We can understand its value and availability and be open to the moments of intimacy that present themselves. We can allow such moments to deepen between us and our patient respectfully, without running away or changing the subject. We are able to do so with less trepidation if we have pondered meaning and developed our inner self.

"I feel so ashamed that nothing Sam is doing is making me feel better," Becky confessed. She was pregnant with their first child and Sam was trying to find a house for them. "They're all so depressing and dark; something about them looks like people's lives are shriveling up, that I would die inside them."

I listened, wondering about depression of course, but hearing something more. "Where do you picture feeling peace?"

"Inside light, trees, sun…"

"Like your poems, the ones you wrote by the water…"

"Yes."

"Nature vitalizes you."

"Yes!" Becky started crying. "But that feels so picky, so petty of me. Why can't I be happy in the houses Sam is finding for me?"

I told Becky a story of my late godmother, an artist with a generous heart and gut-deep sensibilities. When she walked into a room where the colors' tones weren't in harmony, she felt literally sick to her stomach. Her nausea was an involuntary spasm; she wasn't being "picky." When retirement brought a move, her husband searched high and low for the right house in their new city. He knew she could not endure physically unless something about the home's harmonies sung. He found the place.

Becky was riveted. "This makes me feel normal," she said. "It gives me hope."

"Your consciousness, your sensibilities, Becky, live in a place outside of words. You feel the energy in places; you can't help that. You crave an environment that sings what you feel inside and express in your poems." I thought then of a passage I had read that morning by McGilchrist (2009) and pulled it up to read to Becky.

> The forces of wind and gravitation that end up instantiated as a wave in water do not depend on water for their being, only for their expression at that moment as a wave. They exist apart from—in a sense, above and behind—the water in which they are instantiated, and would carry on existing if the water were not there, though then they would be deprived of their form of expression as that particular wave. Similarly, I believe, it may be that consciousness does not depend on a brain for its existence: just, in the absence of a brain, it is deprived of its expression as that particular mind. (p. 465)

As I read the passage aloud I started worrying that it was way more abstruse than I'd remembered it and feared I might be wobbling off Becky's path onto my own. However, when I finished, Becky was touched to tears. "This speaks to me like a poem. It reminds me of a quote by John Muir, 'The sun shines not on us but in us.'"

It was my turn to be touched by Becky's gift back to me. "Yes. The sun is in you. It speaks. Through your craving for a house with light in it. Through your poetry."

"I want to take my poetry journal to the hospital with me when I deliver; it'll help me feel more my whole self," Becky responded.

In retrospect, our connection, ferried by my godmother, McGilchrist, and Muir, was an unplanned moment of transport. Becky and I connected, and our connection formed a passageway for Becky to a deeper connection with herself. She felt her own essence through my feeling it and speaking it back to her. As she joined with her inner being instead of squirming ashamedly inside it, she felt as she put it, her "whole self." Becky and her husband found a home full of natural light and surrounded by trees. Becky's work to let in, understand, and embrace her whole self continued.

Novelist Frances de Pontes Peebles once said, "Ideas are sparks of life. We must give them energy or they flicker out" (personal communication, October 14, 2018). Our patients are filled with sparks of life. When we see those sparks and give them the energy of our consciousness, they grow and glow.

Helping Patients Develop Meaning

> Things fall apart; the centre cannot hold;
> Mere anarchy is loosed upon the world,
> -Yeats, *The Second Coming*

Meaning is the frame that holds us in place; when meaning dissolves foreboding creeps in. Without meaning our stomachs sicken in free-fall as if plunging 400 feet at a 90-degree angle down through the clockwise spiral of a steel roller-coaster (New Jersey's *Kingda Ka*). Yeats (1920) captured this feeling in his poem *The Second Coming*. Written post-World War I, it evoked the sensation that the world was wobbling on its axis and the things people thought were firmly in place were now flying apart without rhyme or reason.

Following a traumatic event, re-establishing meaning is one of two things correlated with recovery. Trauma shatters assumptions about the world, ourselves, and how other people are going to act (Janoff-Bulman, 1985). To recover, we must build sense into the cruelty of the experience in a way that allows us to walk through life without being constantly vigilant against attack or neglect. Infants need structure and routine to organize their bodily rhythms. Adults need a corresponding ideational structure to steady their mind-body rhythms. That organizing ideational structure is our explanations for what keeps the world running sanely and what our role is in it. As Joseph Campbell (1988) put it, "What we are looking for is a way of experiencing the world that will open to us the transcendent that informs it, and at the same time forms ourselves within it...That is what the soul asks for" (p. 53).

Some find resonating explanations in religion. Others construct meaning from philosophy, science, art, or nature. The source or particular explanation is less important than that there is some form of explanation. Being cognizant of the personal meaning we make out of being alive is essential to mental health.

Discussing our patient's frame of meaning can be a natural conversation in psychotherapy despite its esoteric aura. We can ask our patient about it as directly and matter of factly as we ask about her tearfulness, shifts of topic, silences, or confusing statements. We stay interested. We listen not simply to what she says explicitly but also to what she shows us in how she lives and what she spends her time and money on. Yapko (2009) points out that sometimes what people think and say they believe in does not match how they apportion their lives. How one acts reflects what she values more than her statements do. Noticing discrepancies between statements and actions can be an eye-opening conversation starter. It is also an opportunity for our patient to think consciously about what she truly wants to honor in her life and how to choose that.

In discussing meaning, we listen for how our patient feels valuable, what she feels her purpose in life is, and where and how she feels she fits into the larger webs of life's connections.

Value

Feeling we are worth something is the core of emotional well-being. Using comparisons—I'm worth more than you because I did something better than you—as the foundation for self-worth is a precarious base. Fiske (2011) presents data showing how fickle status, competitive hierarchies, and power are. In contrast, forming "a consciousness of one's inner value, anchored in higher, more spiritual things ... cannot be shaken" (Frankl, 1963, p. 99).

Patients who were emotionally bruised and battered at young ages must rebuild a healthy sense of personal value. Their beliefs about themselves were warped during development by distorted perceptions and projections from other people. Those who were doted upon blindly as they grew, being neither seen realistically nor held accountable for poor behavior, have a different challenge. They must learn as adults to separate adulation from worth. They must learn how to construct an inner worth and hold onto it while they *earn* external merits, rather than feel entitled to them.

Listen for whether or not your patient feels she holds value and what she believes makes herself and others valuable. You'll hear answers in the adjectives she uses when describing herself and others and in what she regularly admires or derides. Inquire with interest into her reasoning if she calls herself stupid or describes someone else as brilliant or lucky. Upend her assumptions. Was she "stupid" or did she make a mistake? Does what she did merit hating herself or could she consider being dis-appointed? Can she appreciate determination and courage instead of attaching her value to an outcome? Can she forgive herself and feel compassion for her stumbles?

Purpose

Frankl (1963) quotes Nietzsche as saying, "He who has a *why* to live for can bear with almost any *how*" (p. 121). The why is our purpose. Purpose doesn't pre-exist; we construct it.

Frankl (1963) was adept at guiding people to crafting their purpose. Sometimes he would ask people to consider what they believed life de-manded of them either now or in the future. What was it that only they could do that would need being done. No life can be replicated, no person replaced, Frankl would say. He would have a patient imagine lying on her death bed years from now and looking back over her life. He would ask her what she thought about the life she was picturing having lived. From there patients would be guided to the purpose they discerned themselves having had. Ask your patient what she believes her purpose is. If she feels disheartened about not having any purpose or is simply confused by the idea, ask if she is or ever has been glad to be alive. If so, why. Notice when she lights up with pride or joy and ask what made her mood change just then. Watch and listen for what her gifts are. What do people thank her for doing? Is anyone or anything better off for her having been here? If she knew she had one year to live, what would she do?

Purpose evolves as we age and as circumstances change. People need to reconsider their purpose at the junctures of new developmental stages. This is where many get stuck. For example, Ester struggled for an answer when I asked her what her reason was now for fighting. Her purpose through life had been to fight and win, to defy odds and hold triumph up as proof of her worth. Now that she couldn't be sure of beating this third cancer back I felt her struggle to define what her purpose was. We wrestled together to figure it out; sometimes she turned on me, wrestling with me because of what she felt was my effrontery in exposing this question. Ester was so much more than her fighting. But it was difficult for her to open up to the new forms her purpose might take. We all need a large dollop of humility and flexibility when life's changes require us to rethink our purpose, whether those changes are retirement, staying home to raise children, moving to a new city, or being struck with severe illness like Ester's. Tragically, humility and flexibility were not Ester's strengths. She floundered.

Connections

Connections infuse us with vital life energy. As humans learned globally during the Covid-19 pandemic quarantine, there is no substitute for the nourishment of in-person vibrancy. Without it we feel the color and pulse of living drain away.

Infusions of life energy come not only from people but also from nature and animals. With whom does our patient exchange caring? Whom does she notice, watch and engage with? Within what webs of community does she feel threaded and attached? For one patient it was her tiny pet mice. For another, it was the birds at her feeder. For Mary Oliver (2016), the poet, it was in part her beloved bogs, swamps, and woods on Cape Cod, and the kinship she felt with certain treasured poets whose words she held close to her. "I go nowhere, I arrive nowhere without them. With them I live my life, with them I enter the event" (p. 57).

If the threads connecting your patient to life's energy have thinned, can she strengthen their weave through such gestures as reciprocating to a neighbor who shares flower seeds, attending a book group at the local library, logging-in to an online yoga group, or pausing to greet the dogs on her morning walks? If not, can connection begin with you, the therapist, however tentatively with you she may share the details of her life?

Traits Worth Investing In

Certain personal traits strengthen our ability to construct and maintain durable meaning. When we nurture these traits in ourselves, as early in life as possible, we invest in our emotional future.

Humility and Flexibility

I mentioned Ester's low reserves of humility and flexibility. By humility, I mean accepting that we are not always right and don't always know, without either truth shaking our self-worth. By flexibility, I mean welcoming new facts and new points of view as interesting rather than as threats. Humility and flexibility are key to resilience.

As we discussed in Chapter 5, even though we may be wired to crave certainty, security, and predictability, the future is impossible to know. There is an infinite number of continuously morphing dynamics determining that future. Trying to cope by anticipating what will happen next is thus a tenuous way to adapt. We need to center our security on a sturdier principle.

To do so let's look again at the aerodynamic definition of stability. Stability for an aircraft is not flying through gusts of wind with wings continuously out straight. It is the capacity to *return to center* after the wings have tilted with the unexpected gusts. The same holds true for people. Stability is not the ability to never feel disrupted or ruffled; it is the ability to return to equilibrium after disruptions. A stable construction of meaning builds on the strength of our center—our spiritual core—when we get disrupted, not on achieving a particular outcome or a fortress of plans that we think will guarantee not being caught off guard. When hit by change we lean into our center first, rather than flailing for answers outside ourselves. To strengthen our center we strengthen our abilities to slow down, to face awareness of the truths in front of us, to think even while feeling, and to form responses that we treat as legitimate no matter how others are responding.

It is worth repeating: the equilibrium of feeling centered cannot be sustained continuously. On a hard day, it is lost and returned to hundreds of times. That's reality, not mental illness.

Agency

Prolonged helplessness is a traumatizing thing. Having agency, i.e., having something active and effective to do vs. being helpless, can mean the difference between developing or not developing PTSD after a threatening event.

Seligman's beagles (Seligman, 1972; Seligman & Maier, 1967) painfully demonstrated this point. In an elaborately designed series of experiments, 25–29 pound dogs were given significant shocks to their paws, randomly timed, for 30 seconds, up to 64 times. One group of dogs could, by moving their heads, hit panels situated on both sides of their heads, and when they hit either panel the shock stopped immediately. A second group had the same panels near their heads but hitting them did nothing to stop the shock. The dogs who had no control over the shocks fell into lassitude, and were subsequently unable to figure out, in a different experimental set-up, that if they simply jumped over a small barrier, they could escape the metallic floor that was shocking them. In contrast, the first group who had been able to stop the shocks by hitting the panels figured out quite quickly how to jump the new barrier to stop the shocks. Notwithstanding the controversiality of this experimental approach, its key finding has been replicated in different experimental designs with cats, rats, fish, and people: helplessness is learned. Self-efficacy is learned. Being able to do something about one's circumstances emboldens a person to keep battling forward.

Frankl (1963) saw the effects loss of sense of agency had for prisoners in Nazi concentration camps. As a physician, he witnessed fellow inmates succumb to typhus after losing their sense of agency. Frankl believed that the loss of hope brought on by feeling there is nothing one can do weakens the immune system.

Fiske (2011) viewed the importance of agency from a societal angle. When people lose access to upward mobility, a domino effect of downwardly spiraling events ensues. Violence increases, health problems increase, and quality of life declines, independent of effects from low income. The health problems are called "weathering" (Geronimus et al., 2019; Jones et al., 2019), which is a gradual breakdown of the body over time from the chronic hopelessness, uncertainty, and anger that losing agency begets. It is just as Frankl intuited.

The hazardous effects of chronic helplessness are clear and the fact that self-efficacy is learned and builds on itself is clear. In the face of this knowledge, it makes sense to strengthen agency in our patients. Since we know that for self-efficacy to be learned it must be physically experienced, we want to support our patients' actions, not just their talking and thinking. "Actions" could be speaking directly with a boyfriend about what is making them unhappy. It could be writing an effective email to a committee, completing a difficult project, or building muscle strength in a gym. It could be a patient mustering her courage to tell us directly about her disappointment in us. We want to identify opportunities in our patient's life to experience efficacy and emphasize both her effort and her moments of efficacy until she begins noticing and appreciating both herself.

Strengthening one's sense of agency is not about strengthening one's belief that she can control outcome. Ronald Niebuhr famously prayed, "God grant me the serenity to accept the things I cannot change, the courage to change the things I can and the wisdom to know the difference." Niebuhr linked agency with acceptance. It was a brilliant equation. Take responsibility and gather courage to work for what you can affect. Dare to fail. Don't see external circumstances and other people as controlling everything that happens to you. At the same time, recognize that you don't have the power to make all aspects of everything you believe in or envision happen. If you don't reach your goals, it does not follow that you "failed." You succeeded in endeavoring. You probably grew in unintended ways by doing so.

Holding to Neibuhr's balance is not easy. I think back to my mentor, Irv Rosen, who once told me at Menninger when I struggled over a tragic patient outcome, "'It's not my fault,' says the narcissist. 'It's all my fault,' says the narcissist." At the time his comment to me was mind-bending. It took years to eventually wrap my brain around it. While trying to comprehend it I learned firsthand how neurologically obstinate the pull to think in extremes can be. When I would inch toward pondering my blame, I became too horrified to think I'd done anything for which I was culpable. Then I would reassure myself I'd done nothing remiss, but the gnawing in my stomach told me that was impossible. Blame dropped over me like a shroud. Nothing about this ping-ponging back and forth was productive; it led me to no insights and no learning that would change my behavior going forward. It was only through staying still in the middle that I began to move forward. In the middle, I was forced to face my responsibility and, simultaneously, bear the reality of my limitations. I had contributed to *and* had not been able to control the outcome. This proved to be uncomfortable, but it was the only place from which I could learn. I began outlining what had been my blind spots. I shouldered the work of repairing my shortcomings. I took hold of the understanding that I cannot change others' feelings, thoughts, and actions, however, I can monitor my own, speak clearly what I see, and commit to being present and active with what I believe is important. I can keep striving.

Grieving and Gratitude

Accepting limitations—in ourselves, in others, when falling short of our dreams, when feeling keen disappointment in being unable to accomplish a goal—leads us to grieving. Grieving helps unstick us from holding on to what we wished had happened so that we are freed to move forward into what can happen now. Growth brings loss. The cicada sheds its exoskeleton to create room for its wings. A mother feels pangs as her baby wiggles out of her arms to walk instead of cuddle. In psychotherapy, when we grow, we lose beliefs we clung to in order to get by. We lose unquestioned trust in people who did not deserve our trust, and then we feel alone and unsure about what is left. We slam into moments of sharp realization that there are things we cannot reach and cannot undo. The scales fall from our eyes and we see the opportunities lost from poor choices we made in the past or robbed from us by the poor behavior of others.

We must make meaning of such loss. If we cannot bear to feel its ache we stay stuck. To shed it is to grieve. Grieving is not giving up. It is the excretion of the pain, the wanting, and the awareness of not-going-to-have. Grieving is the full-out weeping that is beyond words. Grieving does not settle softly like sadness, nor is it the locked tomb of depression. Grieving is fresh, and alive. Words are secondary; they come only in grieving's wake. We help our patient through grieving by staying with her and witnessing the reality of the loss. If we can bear her loss as real and refrain from trying to make her "feel better," we help her move through it. Grieving is a true saying-goodbye. It is not canceling or ghosting; it is taking a final, somber look as one turns and slowly walks out the door.

Gratitude stands ready as grieving ebbs. It helps us find the gift inside the tragedy. Gratitude provides a balm for the rawness grieving leaves. We acknowledge what was good (if that is true) inside a bad situation, which helps us emerge with something, rather than with nothing.

Gratitude also keeps us balanced in life. In a culture driven by market economics, we are vulnerable to absorbing messaging that wants are really needs. The long-term effect of that refrain is a chronic, niggling background dissatisfaction with what we have. An antidote to that dissatisfaction is cultivating gratitude. Gratitude may begin with a list of words, but it soaks in best if we cultivate it as a *feeling*. It is that well-being and warmth that radiate from unplanned moments of human kindness, the contentment from a job completed, the wonder of leaves turning color and dappled by drops of sun. Gratitude helps us weather losses. It averts the slow slide into emptiness that a life built around acquisition can bring. Gratitude does not deny the reality of pain; it walks shoulder to shoulder with it. It is not always easy to feel gratitude. It is a practice.

Curiosity

The same mentor who bent my mind at an early age with his statement about blame hit home again on a different occasion when he reflected about loss. He quoted from T.H. White (1958/1987):

> "The best thing for being sad," replied Merlyn, beginning to puff and blow, "is to learn something. That's the only thing that never fails. You may grow old and trembling in your anatomies, you may lie awake at night listening to the disorder of your veins, you may miss your only love, you may see the world about you devastated by evil lunatics, or know your honour trampled in the sewers of baser minds. There is only one thing for it then—to learn. Learn why the world wags and what wags it. That is the only thing which the mind can never exhaust, never alienate, never be tortured by, never fear or distrust, and never dream of regretting. Learning is the only thing for you. Look what a lot of things there are to learn." (p. 183)

Rosen, through T.H. White, was communicating that being curious and pursuing learning moves us beyond loss into something larger than ourselves. Curiosity is a lever that pries us out of being stuck and pulls us out of the hole that loss can sink us into. Perhaps it is no accident that to pry means to look or inquire closely or curiously.

Plato

I want to end this section with 2,500-year-old wisdom. Traits that have stood such a test of time are worth perpetuating a while longer. In Book

IV of *The Republic*, Plato (360 B.C.E./1991) put forth what he considered to be the virtues he believed to be core to an ethical and happy life. They are:

Courage.
Justice.
Wisdom.
Moderation.

Plato observed that the well-being of a society mirrors the degree to which its individuals have invested in these virtues. Put differently, developing our inner character betters not only ourselves, but it lifts up the people and community around us as well. There is a Chinese proverb of unknown origin that speaks the same:

> If there is light in the soul, there is beauty in the person. If there is beauty in the person, there is harmony in the home. If there is harmony in the home, there is order in the nation. If there is order in the nation, there is peace in the world.

In contemplating Plato's list, I am reminded how having a conscience with its accompanying remorse when we have done something wrong, and considering the well-being of others not just that of ourselves, are evidence of psychological maturation (Peebles, 2012). They are neither pointless, impractical, nor outmoded.

In contemplating this chapter, I pondered how we are in need of holding onto some conception of soul in psychotherapy, one that connects us to the eternal or the transcendent, whatever that may be.

Finding Our Own Meaning As Therapists

Therapists need a sense of meaning too.

"At the heart of our work," said Bruno Bettelheim (1972), "is not any particular knowledge or any procedure as such, but *an inner attitude to life* and to those caught up in its struggle" (p. 11, emphasis added). Our own inner attitude and purpose, our ideas about connections, and our thoughts about our value will seep into our work. It will affect how our faces move in response to what our patient just said or did. It will affect what we pick to respond to amidst the paragraphs she just spoke. It will determine how we treat her implicitly as a person. We have a responsibility to be conscious of what our beliefs are.

A therapist's underlying sense of purpose is highly personal. Each therapist's construction is different.

The Meaning We Create

Most psychotherapists come into the field not only because of aptitude. They are also motivated to heal something in themselves or in their original families. This is not just true for psychotherapists; the urge to fix something motivates many professional choices. This is not a shameful truth; it is a testament to the human spirit. We strive consciously or unconsciously to better conditions through passing on something more than what we received.

To the extent possible, it is important as psychotherapists to learn what we are unconsciously trying to heal in ourselves so we can work out our original battles in our personal psychotherapy or within ourselves, not through our patients. In the best of worlds, the lessons we learn from working out our own issues can be gifted to our patients.

Meaning on the other hand is slightly different from motivation. Meaning concerns the larger values that guide our work. It forms our true north.

Childhood Kernels

Daniel Kahneman (Kahneman, 2011; Tippett, 2017) is unambiguous about the fact that as much as we'd like to think we select our values through conscious decision and rational thought, we do not. Our values embed in us from the day we are born, unchosen and un-worded, from our community, our family, and our cultural context.

I believe it is also true that we can mature those childhood kernels into adult values and meaning if we consciously examine our original influences and intentionally choose to expand, correct, override and otherwise evolve them. Doing so requires the humility and intellectual security to realize our original influences are not necessarily The Only Truth. They are merely the water *we* happened to grow up swimming in. Once we become aware of our childhood influences, we are freer to choose practicing those we want to live by.

To illustrate this process let me offer small snippets of a few childhood influences on me and what they were later mixed with to form aspects of my Meaning.

My mother was a walking dispenser of aphorisms. She spoke them to me; she rallied herself with them; she used them when commentating on others. Her sayings seeped into me. "Where there's a will there's a way; A job worth doing is worth doing well; Always leave a place better than how you found it; Blessed are the peacemakers; Don't just stand there, ask what can I do to help; (and her frequent Little Blue Engine chant) I think I can, I think I can; I thought I could, I thought I could!" She counted *Aesop's Fables* and *The Lives of the Saints* among the world's best educators and she supplied me amply with various versions of both.

We were also a devoutly religious family. We didn't just eat fish on Fridays with the other Catholics. We had tiny holy water fonts affixed to the wall outside each bedroom and kneeled for family Rosaries weekly in the living room lit by flickering vigil lights. I knelt as well through Catholic Mass *daily*, at 6:15 am, beginning as a little girl of five or six alongside my father.

I have not practiced religion since college, but its mysteries and values embedded in me. One of the abundance of lessons that stuck was the Parable of the Talents (Matthew 25: 14–30). The child's version is there was a Master who had three servants. He was due to go off on an extended business trip and decided to test his servants' mettle while gone. He gave one 5 Talents (conservatively estimated to be approximately $150,000 in today's dollars); another, 2 Talents, and the third 1 Talent. Upon his return, he called in each servant and asked for a reckoning. The first two had invested their monies in different goods and doubled what they were given. The Master was pleased with their industry. The third thought it a good idea to pre-serve and not lose his money so he wrapped it up and buried it in the ground; thus, he had only the same amount to show when Master returned. This servant was chastised for doing nothing with what he was given. I was riveted by this parable. What I understood was that I had to figure out how to make my talents grow, not bury them. My aim was unquestionably fed by my mother's repetition of, "A job worth doing is worth doing well."

A second religious remnant was a prayer ascribed to St Francis of Assisi, the 12th-century patron saint of creatures and nature, a fact which endeared him to me from the start. He was frequently depicted with birds resting on his arms, shoulders, and head. What was there not to like? St. Francis said (excerpts):

Lord, make me an instrument of your peace
Where there is hatred, let me sow love
Where there is injury, pardon
Where there is doubt, faith
Where there is despair, hope
Where there is darkness, light
And where there is sadness, joy.

O Divine Master, grant that I may
Not so much seek to be consoled as to console,
To be understood, as to understand,
To be loved, as to love.
For it is in giving that we receive,
And it's in pardoning that we are pardoned,

It is an interesting coincidence that years later I chose to attend Wellesley College, that happened to have as its motto, "non minstrari sed ministrare," not to be ministered unto but to minister.

Adult Meaning

Years of supervision, personal therapy, watching people, and living taught me new lessons, ones I used to knead together with those early influences to fashion my adult formula for Meaning. My childhood kernels clearly flavor the mix strongly. What I can do is be as mindful as possible of maturing their flavor into something more complex and of my choosing.

I held to my mother's can-do spirit ("Where there's a will there's a way"), but I folded into it the reality of my limitations. When my husband was called to war when our first child turned three months old, despite my resourcefulness there was no way to will the government to return him to me nor permit me to travel to where he was. You, the reader, might have been blessed with that awareness without having to test it out, but this Little Engine had to learn the hard way. Determination is a fine quality but it must be leavened with realism and drained of the kind of zeal that needlessly depletes energy and obstructs one's ability to pivot away from goals that are not possible. This understanding has been important for me in working with patients.

St. Francis' altruism was and is inspirational, but toiling in my profession with difficult patients, making my way through adult relationships, and scrutinizing the cultural context of female roles taught me that healthy, mature relationships are mutual and reciprocal not endlessly selfless (Peebles-Kleiger, 2001). As important as understanding, consoling, and loving is in this world, it is necessary to seek being understood, consoled, and loved as well. This value reflects itself in psychotherapy when I ask patients to share with me the responsibility for maintaining the therapeutic alliance, guarding their safety, and achieving their goals.

Those first two snippets are small samples of what makes me feel valuable in life; I'll need to continue adjusting these as I move into new developmental junctures.

This last snippet touches upon purpose. My mother's instruction to leave places better than I found them hit that sweet spot of my intrinsic nature. It germinated inside the contemplative spaces I was forced into as a child by the directives around me toward spiritual devotion. I've filled it out with later learning. For example, the Quakers have a saying from their founder George Fox, "There is that of God within every man." God here is understood broadly as goodness or "light," and Quakers look for these sparks of light within every person, seeking to elicit the "light" from within and hold people "in the light," as ways of bringing out the unique goodness in each person. This same sensibility is found in Buber's writings. Buber sought to substantiate people, bring into them their own feeling of existence through "encountering" or seeing them fully. We can talk about such things as humanistic ideology. I am describing them here as aspects of my sense of purpose. I feel I contribute to this world by offering a relationship in which a person can find once again the parts of themselves splintered off through accommodations to danger and shame. They can retrieve them, eventually embrace them, and through doing so experience their wholeness, their creative multiplicity.

What made the Star Wars cinematic opera the classic that it became is the universality of the eternal battle between forces of light (transcendent creating) and forces of darkness (descendent destruction). It is an endless struggle, the point of which seems merely to uphold the balance in the universe. Those saints whose lives I read as a child were striving, just as Obi Wan Kenobi strived, to bring light into the world. Campbell (Campbell et al., 1988) said that light represents transformation and, "At the darkest moment comes the light" (p. 39). This theme is eternal. In one session, Becky asked me what I felt my purpose was. I answered, "To bring light into the world, to help people find the light within themselves. Helping people in psychotherapy to me is like sending little sparks of light, little armies of goodness out into the world to counterbalance and battle with the forces of darkness."

My answers are not yours. These ideas are not offered as prescriptions. They are shared simply as examples of one person's process. I open them up to you as a way of inviting you to reflect on and engage with shaping your own.

End Thoughts

I'll end this chapter, and this book, with a story from Ben who was in the process of ending his psychotherapy with me.

Ben searched for words. "It's a paradox," he said. "With you, in this relationship, I feel that connection, that feeling that you're right there. You're listening. I appreciate that you've stayed and not tossed me off or turned cold when I got upset with you. This is the thing we talked about in my church study group. How 'God' isn't a creature or a being, it's more all around us, like goodness. For me that goodness is connection, connection that's real between people. It's a nutrient for me. It's what most touches me in life."

"And I have that with you. But, and this makes me sad saying this, I feel at the same time like I'm ready to move on, or move forward. I don't know why this image is coming to my mind—it doesn't match how I feel, but I'm seeing a pair of old jeans. They're ripped and worn, but they've fit so well and felt so right. I can't just throw them out." Ben paused for several seconds. "But I'm ready for a new pair, you know?"

I did know, and I welcomed the image of the jeans. I was grateful for Ben's trust in me and for speaking that image even though he felt like it "didn't match" his feelings. In truth, it did, and better than he expected.

"Yeah, there's something about that pair of jeans," I said. "You've grown out of them, but the feel of their good fit will always stay inside you. And you can take some pieces of those jeans and form something of your own, something you'll bring inside your own home, something you will give to your children."

Ben teared up. "Yes," he said. "I will."

"Your car goes where your eyes go," Garth Stein (2008) wrote in *The Art of Racing in the Rain*. Where your heart looks, so goes your impact in psychotherapy, whatever your theoretical intent. Take care to place your heart where you want it to be. Help your patients leave psychotherapy a little more mindful of where they want their hearts to be too. When psychotherapy feels stuck, finding the road again is more about where you look and how you are looking than the kind of car you are driving. The right turn of the wheels will follow.

References

Aftab, A. (2020, July 29). Psychoanalysis and the re-enchantment of psychiatry: Jonathan Shedler, PhD. *Psychiatric Times*. https://www.psychiatrictimes.com/view/psychoanalysis-re-enchantment-psychiatry-jonathan-shedler-phd

Bettelheim, B. (1972). *The empty fortress: Infantile autism and the birth of the self*. New York, NY: The Free Press, a Division of Simon & Schuster Inc.

Campbell, J., Moyers, B.D., & Flowers, B.S. (1988). *The power of myth*. New York, NY: Anchor Books.

Casals, P. (1970). *Joys and sorrows: Reflections by Pablo Casals as told to Albert E. Kahn*. New York, NY: Simon and Schuster.

Fiske, S.T. (2011). *Envy up, scorn down*. New York, NY: Russell Sage Foundation.

Frankl, V. (1963). *Man's search for meaning*. New York, NY: Washington Square Press, Inc.

Geronimus, A.T., Bound, J., Waidmann, T.A., Rodriguez, J., & Timpe, B. (2019). Weathering, drugs, and whack-a-Mole: Fundamental and proximate causes of widening educational inequity in U.S. life expectancy by sex and race, 1990–2015. *Journal of Health and Social Behavior, 60*(2), 222–239.

Hope, A.E., & Sugarman, L.I. (2015). Orienting hypnosis. *American Journal of Clinical Hypnosis, 57*(3), 212–229.

Janoff-Bulman, R. (1985). The aftermath of victimization: Rebuilding shattered assumptions. In C.R. Figley (Ed.), *Trauma and its wake, Volume I: The study and treatment of post-traumatic stress disorder* (pp. 15–35). New York, NY: Brunner/Mazel.

Jones, N.L., Gilman, S.E., Cheng, T.L., Drury, S.S., Hill, C.V., & Geronimus, A.T. (2019). Life course approaches to the causes of health disparities. *American Journal of Public Health, 109*(S1), S48–S55.

Kahneman, D. (2011). *Thinking, fast and slow*. New York, NY: Farrar, Straus and Giroux.

Lewis, S. (2014). *The rise: Creativity, the gift of failure, and the search for mastery*. New York, NY: Simon & Schuster.

McGilchrist, I. (2009). *The master and his emissary*. New Haven, CT: Yale University Press.

Oliver, M. (2016). *Upstream: Selected essays*. New York, NY: Penguin Press.

Peebles, M.J. (2012). *Beginnings: The art and science of planning psychotherapy* (2nd ed.). New York, NY: Routledge Press.

Peebles-Kleiger, M.J. (2001). The little engine that could. In S. Kahn & E. Fromm (Eds.), *Changes in the therapist: A casebook* (pp. 133–148). Hillsdale, NJ: Lawrence Erlbaum.

Plato (1991). *The republic* (B. Jowett, trans.). New York, NY: Vintage Books. (Original work 360 B. C. E.)

Seligman, M. (1972). Learned helplessness. *Annual Review of Medicine, 23*, 407–412.

Seligman, M., & Maier, S. (1967). Failure to escape traumatic shock. *Journal of Experimental Psychology, 74*(1), 1–9.

Shedler, J. (2010). The efficacy of psychodynamic psychotherapy. *American Psychologist, 65*(2), 98–109.

Stein, G. (2008). *The art of racing in the rain*. New York, NY: Harper.

Tippett, K. (Host). (2017, October 5). Daniel Kahneman: Why we contradict ourselves and confound each other [Audio podcast]. In *On being with Krista Tippett*. WNYC Studios. https://onbeing.org/programs/daniel-kahneman-why-we-contradict-ourselves-and-confound-each-other-jan2019/

White, T.H. (1958/1987). *The once and future king*. New York, NY: Penguin Random House.

Yapko, M. (2009). *Depression is contagious: How the most common mood disorder is spreading around the world and how we can stop it*. New York, NY: Free Press, Simon & Schuster, Inc.

Yeats, W.B. (1920, November). The second coming. *The Dial, 69*(5), 466.

Index

Made in the USA
Las Vegas, NV
30 December 2023

83710496R00092